Praise For

Furious Love
A Journey Through the Heart of Grief

"Anybody that has walked the road of grief knows that it's a journey. The story of Zach Morton and his family's journey through grief will grip your heart and bring hope to your life. I look forward to using this as resource for others who are journeying through the loss of someone they love. Thanks Johnny and Carla for reminding us that even in our darkest moments God loves us with a furious love."

—*Brian Bloye*
Lead Pastor
West Ridge Church
Dallas, GA

"I don't know that I have ever read a more candid and loving story about a life that was cut short in some ways. Z-man was amazing. Your family is just as amazing! You say in this book what the rest of us would probably think, but never make public. Well done!"

—*Chan Gailey*
Kansas City Chiefs
Kansas City, Missouri

"If you knew Zach, it wasn't his death that moved you, it was his life. He was such an extraordinary young man, that I sometimes forget how much he wanted to be just like everyone else. As Johnny and Carla share their grief, you get a glimpse of Zach and of the family he left behind. But most importantly, there is no doubt that Zach is whole again, and will spend eternity with the Father"

—*Kevin Brown*
Starting Pitcher
Major League Baseball, Retired

"In the tradition of C. S. Lewis' classic, A Grief Observed, Johnny and Carla Morton have allowed us to join them on their journey through grief following the death of their teenage son, Zach. *Furious Love* is powerful because it is honest and intimate.

Your heart will be moved by this story of love . . . and loss . . . and family . . . and faith. For even as the Mortons have walked through one of the deepest valleys this life has to offer, in Christ they have found God's sovereignty to be a refuge, his grace to be sufficient, and his love to be steadfast.

As a pastor for twenty years, *Furious Love* is a resource I would heartily recommend. I am confident that God will use it to bring help and hope to you if you are making your own journey through grief."

—Tim McCoy, Ph.D.
Senior Pastor
Ingleside Baptist Church
Macon, Georgia

"In this book, Johnny and Carla take us with them on a journey that no parent expects to take. Their raw honesty is refreshing. I highly recommend this book for all parents who have lost a child to death, to the friends who help them through it, and to the professional counselors who encounter hurting people everyday."

—Jerry Dingmore
Senior Pastor
Piedmont Church
Macon, Georgia

"There is great fear of the pain that accompanies a loss, this story shows the raw pain but along side the pain you see God's grace and hope."

—Dr. Kathryn Kemper
Christian Counseling Center
Macon, Georgia

Furious Love

A Journey Through the Heart of Grief

by

Johnny and Carla Morton

Goose River Press
Waldoboro, Maine

Library of Congress Card Number: 2009924493

ISBN: 978-1-59713-076-9

First Printing, 2009

Published by
Goose River Press
3400 Friendship Road
Waldoboro ME 04572
e-mail: gooseriverpress@roadrunner.com
www.gooseriverpress.com

Table of Contents

Forward

In the years I have been doing professional counseling I have witnessed the spectrum of emotions in grieving a loss from death. Often people need assurance that what they are feeling is normal. They want to know if there will ever be light at the end of this dark tunnel of grief.

In *Furious Love,* Johnny & Carla Morton give us the opportunity to witness first hand the grief journey in the loss of their teenage son Zach. Their story is unique because it is not one of reflection, but moment to moment reality. Their story is told from their daily web journal. They have allowed us to see their heart in the rawest moments of despair, pain, anger and questions. We see not only their raw, unfiltered pain, but also the grace of God that sustains them.

Many times we fear the thought of this type of heart wrenching emotion that the death of a child brings. We fear the overwhelming loss and the grief. We fear life being out of control. We have questions that have no answers.

When we read in God's word that He carries us in our darkest moments it is comforting. But, when we share in Johnny and Carla's experience and see that God carried them when they could not go on, we are given hope. We are comforted and given hope that when we walk through the darkest valleys of this life we too will be carried.

People grieve differently. Often a husband and wife will experience difficulty because they are grieving differently and this causes hurt and conflict. Johnny and Carla give us a picture of people grieving differently, but also of being together in their pain. They show us how even against the odds their marriage survived the grief. Johnny and Carla also give us insight into how to give children the freedom to grieve according to their personality and age.

I believe this book will give you hope and comfort. I believe you will see the awesome grace of God poured out on His children. This story is very close and personal to me. I too felt the pain and grief because I am not just a counselor, I'm also a grandmother, and Zach was my grandson.

— *Dr. Kathryn Kemper, PhD*

Acknowledgements

There are so many to thank for helping us make this book become a reality. We so wanted to finish this last honor we could give Zach. Without their help, encouragement, and prayers we could not have finished.

To our Abba, our Sustainer, our Lord & Savior—Thank you for giving us 18 awesome years with Zach! Thank you for carrying us when we could not walk.

To Judy Rocker, our publicist—Thanks for being our friend and pushing us when we wanted to give up.

*To Deborah and **Goose River Press***—Thanks for believing in us and giving us a platform to tell this story.

*To **Caring Bridge***—Thanks for the service you gave to us and thousands of people around the world that have benefited from your service during times of illness.

To our FPD family—You shared our grief and allowed us the time we needed. Thanks for continuing to honor Zach's life!

To our combined families—Words will never be enough to express our gratitude. You loved and supported us the entire journey, from Zach's birth through these last five years. You loved Zach as if he were your own child. You were always there for us. You have loved us through the pain and heartache. We are eternally grateful.

To our parents—We love you! You were a rock of strength and wisdom to us while experiencing your own grief and pain. You were the arms of God wrapped around us.

To Kemper and Cole—We are so proud of you! You made us laugh when we wanted to cry. You gave us a reason to go on through the pain and grief. You are our trophies of grace. We love you more than you will ever know!

To Zachary King Morton—What a privilege and honor it is to be your parents. You taught us what is most important in life. We can't wait to see you!

Preface

I first heard the term "the furious love of God" in one of Brennan Manning's books. It struck a chord in my soul. When most people think of the love of God, the image I believe they see most often is of a warm, gentle, tender, kind of love. Images of God's comfort and care are what most people see. It is why they struggle so when things don't go the way they would like. They want God's love to be a warm embrace; strong arms that will protect them from all hurt.

Sometimes God's love is like that, but the greatest example of God's love was anything but sweet and gentle. When Jesus died on the Cross, it was the clearest picture of God's love for us we will ever see. It was a furious love and that is the love of God that Carla and I have experienced most of our marriage. Nothing has been easy. From the beginning, God has used the turmoil of life, especially the birth of our first born in 1985, to mold us into His trophies of grace. When God gave us Zach, He forced us into positions where we had no choice but to abandon ourselves to Him.

Before Zach was born, Carla and I had dedicated him to God. We had been married for two years; I was serving in my first church as a youth pastor and Carla was a registered nurse. We had all the dreams young couples have as they are starting out. With the innocence of youth, we eagerly awaited the arrival of our first child.

On September 18, 1985, Zachary King Morton came into the world. We were ecstatic. Our joy soon turned to fear though as the doctors told us they suspected Zach had pneumonia and needed to be transferred to another hospital. The fear that gripped us soon turned to despair when the doctor told us, "It's his heart."

Zach was diagnosed with a congenital heart defect called Tetralogy of Fallot. His heart had multiple defects, the most serious of which was the absence of the pulmonary artery to carry blood to his lungs. After two desperate surgeries in his first 18 months, Zach was alive, but he had a heart defect that needed correction and two lungs damaged by the surgeries.

All of our dreams of a normal life were crushed. Nothing would ever be routine again. Our lives were filled with visits to the doctor and emergency room, endless treatments, huge medical bills, and very little hope that Zach would ever live a normal life. The doctors were not sure Zach would live at all. In spite of the obstacles he faced, Zach grew into an extraordinary young man with a deep love for God, his family and friends, for sports, and for life itself.

Zach grew up in a close knit family surrounded by his two younger brothers, grandparents, numerous aunts, uncles, and cousins. Zach's brother, Kemper, grew into the athlete Zach dreamed to be, but never experienced because of his physical limitations. Cole, Zach's youngest brother, shared a special bond with Zach as he, too, was born with a defective heart.

Zach loved all sports. He hoped to be a coach someday since his frail body would not let him play the sports he so loved. Zach got his nickname, "Z-man," when he started calling a local radio talk show when he was 15. The radio show was live each week during football season. Zach called on a regular basis and they ended up dubbing him "Z-man" and getting his "upset special" of the week. The nickname stuck and he was affectionately called "Z-man" at school and across the community.

For years, Zach defied the expectations of doctors who gave him little chance to live beyond the age of six without a corrective heart surgery. Despite visits to heart surgeons around the country, no one was willing to operate. "It's too risky" they told us. "Just enjoy the time you have left with him."

In 2003, when Zach was 18, we were given our first ray of hope. Dr. Frank Hanley, a world renowned heart surgeon at Lucile Packard Children's Hospital in Palo Alto, California, agreed to evaluate Zach as a candidate for corrective heart surgery. The surgery, if successful, would give Zach a pulmonary artery, provide blood flow to the lungs, and strengthen his weakened heart. Zach would finally have the chance to do some of the things he had dreamed of doing. Barring a miracle from God, this was Zach's last hope. Without surgery, Zach's heart would soon give out.

Zach's life was an example of how God's furious love can produce something awesome. It was never easy. Zach went through pains and discomforts we will probably never know. And yet, it was those very struggles that made Zach the unique person he was. He lived life fully because he knew how fragile it can be. He was determined, I believe, to live every moment to the fullest, because he never knew what tomorrow would bring. It was the furious love of God that made Zach the vessel of love and grace that he was!

As we were preparing for our trip to California, we were introduced to a website called CaringBridge that would allow us to stay connected with family and friends during the train trip to California, Zach's surgery, and his stay in the hospital. CaringBridge started in 1997 with one website to serve one family with a medical crisis. Since then, over 60,000 sites have been created in all fifty states and in fifteen countries around the world. Nine million messages of love, hope and support have been left in CaringBridge guest books. Zach's website, www.caringbridge.org/ga/zach, initially was meant for him, and us, to keep in touch and to hear from family and friends. But on December 5, 2003, after a successful surgery, Zach died and each posting became our journal of grief. For one year we shared our walk through the heart of grief. To our amazement we found that it was helpful to pour out our feelings onto a blank page. We did not have to talk or see anyone but we could share from the rawness of our hearts. It was a safe place to unload. The response was unbelievable. In the following pages we invite you to share in our journey of losing a son and yet, at the same time, experiencing God's *Furious Love.*

Furious Love

A Journey Through the Heart of Grief

"Strength and courage aren't always measured in medals and victories. They are measured in the struggles you overcome. The strongest people aren't always the people who win, but the people who don't give up."

Zachary King Morton
September 18, 1985 – December 5, 2003

Trip to California

"It was cool how they do seating at dinner and lunch on the train because it allows you to meet a different person at each meal."

—Zach

Thursday, November 20, 2003 4:17 PM CST

All systems are a go! In less than 72 hours, Zach and I will be settled on the train and bound for California. Zach went to see his cardiologist in Atlanta, (Dr. David Jones), and had a good report. Everything remains stable and we are set for California. Thanks for all the prayers that have been lifted up on our behalf.

As we read the messages posted on the Caring Bridge website that old friends and new friends have left, we are filled with a mixture of emotions. Pride as we see what great things people say about our son; awe at the number and variety of those who leave messages; encouragement as we see the body of Christ in action as you help bear this burden with us. Thank you for the blessing your kind words and prayers have been to our family!

I thank Him for the peace he has given us as we walk towards the unknown. Please know that your thoughts, messages, and prayers are being felt!   Johnny

Sunday, November 23, 2003 0:36 AM CST

It's only about seven hours until Zach and I depart for California. For so long, this day seemed so far off. Now that it is here, I find myself wondering what changes the next few weeks will bring to our lives. Even as I feel the fear of uncertainty, I remind myself that Zach and our family belong to the One who holds the future in His hands. Zach's surgery date is scheduled for Thursday December 4th. He will still have the heart cath on December 1st as well as all of the pre-op tests. Please pray for Zach's strength and our trip to go smoothly. Thanks. Johnny

Tuesday, November 25, 2003 5:54 PM CST
Zach & Johnny just called. The connection was not good so they kept going in an out. Zach said they had been in the middle of Texas all day and "they don't have any phone coverage at all out here!" It sounds like they are doing fine. I just wanted to say again how overwhelmed we are by such an outpouring of love and prayers. Please know that we love reading each and every posting and have been so blessed by so many. Hopefully Zach and Johnny will be in CA tomorrow and in Palo Alto by tomorrow night. Again, thanks for covering us in prayer. Carla

Thursday, November 27, 2003 0:49 AM CST
We have finally arrived in California. The train was a few hours late but that allowed me to sleep a little later! I'm glad to be stopped, although at times I still feel as though I am moving.
I would like to personally thank everyone who has logged on to follow the trip and signed the guestbook. I know that many people have been and continue to pray for my family and me. Thank You. I know God will do His will this week. I can't wait to be home though. Thanks again, Zach

Friday, November 28, 2003 1:34 AM CST
Happy Thanksgiving to everyone! Hopefully everyone is taking today to recover from overeating. Dad and I did eat turkey; however it was not a normal Thanksgiving meal. We had turkey sandwiches from SUBWAY. Everything was good. We watched football, ate our turkey, and then went to the movie. Pray for my mom as she flies out here Friday. Happy Thanksgiving! Zach

Friday, November 28, 2003 10:03 AM CST
Well, I am headed out in just a little while. I thought I

2

would share one thing that God brought to my mind this morning. I was praying and thinking that I don't know how this will turn out. It may be good, bad or medium. And then it's like God's spirit reminded me that regardless of how I "term" the outcome, it can only be used for our good. *It can't be anything else.* I pray that God will seal that truth in my mind and heart over the next days. (I'm a pretty slow learner at times.....) Again, I am overwhelmed, (we all are), at the outpouring of love, concern, & prayers. Please pray for Kemper and Cole as I leave today. Especially Cole as he is still little, (well he is my baby) and is a little upset with me leaving. Again, I pray a blessing on each of you that are traveling with us in this journey. Carla

Friday, November 28, 2003 11:00 PM CST

My mom made it to California. Everything was very smooth at the airports and in the air. I thought some people might like to hear about some of my train experiences. Here are a few excerpts from my personal journal (Thanks Betsy). Zach

Nov. 24 2:18pm CST

We are in Bayou Vista, LA. Dinner last night was INCREDIBLE!!! Thanks Edward! We had crab cakes and lobster for our appetizers. The desserts were also out of this world! I had bread pudding a la mode with Drunken Monkey ice cream. They also threw in a peanut butter chocolate pie with apricot ice cream. Thanks again to the Lowe's!

8:53pm CST

I'm back in the cabin after watching a movie. We ate supper with a man named Ennis. He needs prayers. Ennis and I got to be pals and he said he is going to try to keep up with me via telephone.

Nov. 25 1:36pm CST

Just ate lunch with a nice couple from Sherman, TX. The best thing on the train is the key lime pie. Texas is very big! It took us nearly 24 hours to cross it. There was an elderly lady who we met the first day on this train who said she wished to pray for me. I agreed and was prayed over right there in the lounge car. The Lord has allowed us to meet some really nice people on the train.

I spent a lot of time in the lounge car just talking to people. One guy is a recovering drug addict who quit 3 years ago. He said he spent the night before reading his Bible so I was encouraged by that. It was cool how they do the seating at dinner and lunch because it allows you to meet a different person every meal.

I spent so much time in the lounge I got to know the lounge manager. At the end when she was thanking everyone for buying snacks from her and wishing everyone a Happy Thanksgiving, she wished me well during my upcoming surgery. It was amazing to see how many people listened to me when I told them the reason for taking a train from GA to CA was for heart surgery. Sorry for being so long winded (which I do a lot). Thanks for the prayers. Zach

P.S. We are going to the Notre Dame Stanford game tomorrow and my dad and I are also going to catch the UGA women's basketball team this Sunday here at Stanford.

Sunday, November 30, 2003 10:49 PM CST

Today was a lot of fun. UGA lost, and, yes, I was hoping they would win even though I am a die-hard Auburn fan. Last night was a lot of fun at the Notre Dame Stanford Game. Notre Dame killed 57-7 but it was fun. It was a whole lot different than being in Auburn, Athens, or even Atlanta. There were more visiting fans than there were for the home team.

Tomorrow will be a long day. We have to leave the hotel by 6:15 am to go check in for the heart cath. We saw a shirt that was just right for me this week, "Wake me when it's over." Pray for my grandparents, Kitty & Larry and my brother, Kemper, as they fly out here on Tuesday. Pray for my aunt Kathy as she will have Cole, my brother, who is still a little whiney. We will let everyone know how the heart cath goes ASAP.

Thanks again for all the love and prayers, Zach

4

P.S. To the basketball teams back at FPD (First Presbyterian Day School), I plan on being back for the Christmas Tournament at the latest! Go VIKINGS!!!

Zach's Decision

Suddenly Zach asked, "Are you asking me if I know that I might die?" I just sat there. "How long have you known?"
—*Carla*

Monday, December 1, 2003 11:53 AM CST

I just wanted to let everyone know our status at this time. They took Zach back for the cath about 8:30 CA time. They said it would probably be several hours. Zach was premeditated so he was sleepy when he left. Johnny & I are wandering around, it's a huge place. We'll post later; hopefully we will have more direction after the heart cath. Carla

Monday, December 1, 2003 3:43 PM CST

After four and one half hours, Zach is back from his cath. The doctor said they were able to get all the information they needed. They also did some of his pre-op testing while he was back in the cath lab. He said as far as he can tell we will proceed with surgery on Thursday. As far as what exact surgery they will perform, Dr. Hanley will make that decision after reviewing the cath results. We will meet with Dr. Hanley on Wednesday morning. We will stay in the hospital for the next 5-6 hours because they used both legs for the cath. Zach will have a few more tests while we are waiting. We should return to the hotel later this evening. Carla
****

During Zach's recovery time the assistant surgeon came to talk to us. He began to explain in "painful" detail what surgical options we might have. He said that the surgeon might be able to do the entire correction in one surgery. If he did that, it would be an extremely long and tedious sur-

6

gery and a two week to three month stay in the hospital. If the surgeon opted for a two step procedure he would do a portion of the repair during the first surgery and then come back months later and complete the repair. The longer the assistant talked the worse things became. I could see that Zach was about to lose it. I was thinking this guy better leave before Zach blows.

After he left I went out to use the phone to call and check on the children. The nurse was going to help Zach up to the bathroom. I was trying to keep it together but was so stressed. I had never fathomed a possible three month stay. What would I do about Christmas? What about the other children? I could not be away that long? What was the right answer? When I returned from the phone call I could hear this deep wailing from the bathroom. Zach was sobbing so loudly that you could hear him all over the unit. It was a cry from a broken heart. He was in such anguish and pain. I lay across the bed and sobbed my own bitter tears. I said, "Why God? Zach has been as faithful as anyone I have ever known. Why does it have to be this hard?" When Zach finally came out, he just kept saying, "I don't want to do this. I want to go home. Please let me go home."

We tried to talk about the fact that to make an informed decision you have to know all of the facts and choices. Zach could decide not to do anything, but he had to know what that choice meant. He had to know what his options were. It was late before Zach could be discharge from the hospital. When they finally said we could go I knew Zach was just dying to get out of there. I went to find Johnny and he was no where to be found. I started getting so mad. I thought I might blow. I was running up and down the halls of this massive medical facility. I had no idea where Johnny had gone. I even had him paged over the loud speaker. I rounded the corner and saw him coming down the hall. I screamed at the top of my lungs. "Where in the Hell have you been?" I thought it was a fairly appropriate response.

We finally left and went to get Zach something to eat. As we sat at the table, all of our emotions were raw. Zach was tired and hurting from the heart cath. We were all emotionally spent. I was trying to find the right words to say to Zach. I needed to make certain he understood that since he was eighteen years old a lot of this decision was his. We could not make it for him. But we had to have all of the facts to make an informed choice. I was trying to figure out how to tell him that if we did not do the surgery he probably did not have a very promising future. I did not want to tell him more than he was ready or needed to hear. I wanted to try and determine what Zach understood about his condition and what his life expectancy might be without any intervention.

All of a sudden Zach said, "Are you asking if I know that I might die?" I just sat there. I said, "How long have you known?" Zach said he had known it since the first time we were in California. He said, "You don't stay in the intensive care unit for two weeks unless you're close to dying." I asked him why he had never said any thing to us about it. He said, "Well, there really wasn't anything to talk about." For two years Zach had known that he almost died and that he might die and he had never mentioned it to anyone.

I spent another restless night. All night I reviewed the options that the assistance doctor had talked about. None of the options seemed good. The prospect of trying to do the correction in one surgery was daunting. The thought of having to come back in 6 months and do it again was equally overwhelming. Not having surgery seemed a definite death sentence. I wrestled all night. Again, I begged God to make it clear. I had no idea what was right.

Tuesday, December 2, 2003 8:40 AM PST

It was a hard night last night. Many tears were shed. As we talked with Zach about the decisions we have to make, we wanted to make sure that he understood the risks of not having surgery, if that is even an option. He understands that no surgery means his heart may soon wear out. Pray that God will allow us to make a decision based on "a spirit of love, power, and a sound mind," not "a spirit of fear." Thanks again for all your prayers. We do feel God's peace. I can't imagine having to go through this without Him!

Zach is overwhelmed with the decision he may face.

Either do the surgery with all the risks and a possible extended stay in California, or go home without doing anything and dealing with that reality. Zach is in a very hard place right now! Please pray for him. Neither option is appealing. Both are scary. For a long time we could protect him from these decisions. We can't anymore. Pray that God will somehow give Zach a peace in all this turmoil. Pray for Carla and me as we watch Zach hurt and try to help him deal with this. The one thing we know is that Zach is where he has always been, in the hands of a loving, sovereign God. It is not always an easy place to be though. Johnny

Tuesday, December 2, 2003 7:21 PM CST

Larry, Kitty, and Kemper have arrived safely. We have not talked much about tomorrow, but it is always there in the back of our mind. I am so thankful that our family has come. Zach needs that strength and comfort God provides through them. Pray for peace and wisdom for us all in the upcoming decisions. Pray that God will make our path clear. We know He is faithful, but the waiting on Him and learning to rest is a hard thing right now! Johnny

Wednesday, December 3, 2003 11:00 PM CST

We walked into the surgeon's (Dr. Hanley) office with much trepidation. The minute we sat down Dr. Hanley looked at Zach and said, "Well, are you ready for surgery?" Zach said, "Well, I don't know." The surgeon went on to explain what he saw as the two options and what his recommendation would be. He explained that he thought the surgery needed to be done in two steps. The first surgery would be the following day. He would try and work on the area that was the most difficult to lay the ground work for a total correction during the second surgery. He explained that this surgery would not require the by-pass machine and he should be out of the hospital in a week. He said that he thought Zach might even get some benefit from the first surgery since his oxygen level might increase which would increase his stamina. Zach asked him what would happen if we did not do anything. He explained that Zach would begin to lose more and more stamina and even the things he could do now would become difficult. He said he might have a few years left without any surgery. He went on to say that with the surgery he thought Zach would have several decades of life. He told Zach, "You will be able to do things after we correct you that you have never been able to do. You will not believe how good you will feel." Zach said, "I would just like to play ball in the yard with my brothers."

I asked what he thought his chances of success were. He said the surgery had a 97% chance of survival. He said even with the second surgery it was probably a 95% chance. I just could not believe what I was hearing. Dr. Haney was so positive and so certain of the course we needed to take. He had absolute confidence. We walked out of the office and got on the elevator. I said to Zach, "Well, what do you think?" He said, "There's really no choice. I have to have the surgery." We spent part of the rest of that day having tests in preparation for the surgery. Zach wanted to drive into San Francisco that night before the surgery. We all tried to make it a fun time. We were scared but also had some distant hope that somehow this time things might be different. Maybe this is what we had been waiting for his whole life. Carla

Wake Me When It's Over

When we first went back to see Zach....he looked so good. He actually looked pink. I even lifted up the covers to see his toes. For the first time in his life they were not blue.

—Carla

The next morning arrived way too early. We dressed in quiet in the hotel room and prepared to go to the hospital. Zach wore the shirt I had gotten him that said, "Wake Me When It's Over." He also wore his school letter jacket. He had hardly taken it off; he was so proud to have received it. We tried not to make saying good-bye too emotional but just sort of see you when you wake up. He looked brave and scared all at the same time. Carla

Thursday, December 4, 2003 9:44 AM CST

They have taken Zach back to surgery. It will be a long day. As we drove to the hospital this morning, I was filled with a myriad of emotions. I was worried about what Zach might be thinking. I was a little fearful, recognizing the risk of death that is always there with a major surgery. I was dreading the moment we see him in ICU with a ventilator, tubes and IV's. Most of all, I was filled with hope that this is the first step of a process that may enable Zach to do so many of the things that the rest of us take for granted. You feel all these things and more, ultimately saying "God, he is in your hands. Take care of Zach, because I know You love him even more than I do." We will post as soon as Zach is out of surgery. Thanks for being there for us! Johnny

11

Thursday, December 4, 2003 4:10 PM CST

The surgery took most of the day. When Dr. Hanley finally came out to talk with us he looked relaxed and very satisfied. He said that Zach had done great. They had been able to do everything they had wanted to do to lay the foundation for a complete repair with the next surgery. He said Zach was as stable as a rock. We thanked him and told him that no one had ever given us any hope in 18 years. This was the first time we had hope and good news. We were thrilled. He told us that we could see Zach in little while after they got him settled in the unit. Carla

Thursday, December 4, 2003 6:46 PM CST

PRAISE GOD!!! HE IS GOOD!!!

Just a short note. I will post more later. Zach is out of surgery and doing great (considering he just came out of 6 1/2 hours of surgery). His surgeon said Zach did great with minimal problems and bleeding. Dr. Hanley was able to do all he wanted to and said Zach should be set up for his next surgery. Zach is in adult ICU, but no visitation problems. Prayer needs now are THANKSGIVING & PRAISE! Also, please pray that his right lung will accept the increased blood flow. We will give more complete information later. Thanks again for all you prayer warriors!!! Amen & Amen!!!!! Johnny
****

When we first went back to see Zach he was still asleep. He looked so good. He actually looked pink. He had not looked pink in years. I even lifted up the covers to see his toes. For the first time in his life his toes were not blue. I could not believe it. We cried and rejoiced. I felt like I was witnessing a healing occur through man's hands but totally ordained by God. It was just amazing. His oxygen saturations were in the 80's. He had not been out of the low 70's or even 60's in years. It was so wonderful. The anesthesiologist was in the room and said what a fine young man he seemed to be. I told him, "I know he is mine but I could not be prouder and he really is a fine young man. He has been remarkable his whole life."

The doctor said, "I could tell that just by talking to him

12

before we put him to sleep."

We had to leave after a few minutes when we returned the next time Zach had his eyes open. I ran over to him and said that it was over and he had done great. He took his hand and held up his index finger to indicate "i" then he put his fist over his heart to represent love and then pointed to me. He had signed I love you. I begin to cry and about laid my body over him in the bed. I told him how proud I was of him and what a joy he had been. I said that I was honored to be his mother. He kept trying to talk around the ventilator. I was trying to guess what he was asking about. He seemed to be asking about my parents. It was time for shift change and I told Zach that we would go and change clothes and be back to spend the night in the waiting room. He seemed to be fairly comfortable when we left.

When we returned they were saying that Zach was having more bleeding from his chest tube than they liked. The surgeon came in about that time and Zach stuck out his hand to the doctor. The surgeon explained that he thought it would be better to take Zach back to surgery and see why he was having so much bleeding from the chest tube. He went on to say that it was not a set back but he thought it would be better to go back in and clean everything out rather than to chase the bleeding all night. He said it would only take a little while and then Zach would be back in the unit. I hated it, but it seemed like the surgeon was still very confident that things were fine. Zach seemed anxious to try and tell me something. He kept trying to talk around the ventilator. I kept trying to guess what he was saying and I was not doing a very good job. He was getting frustrated. I said, "Do you want to write it down?" He nodded yes. I grabbed a paper towel and a pen. Zach wrote on the paper. Tell K & C that I love them. (That stood for Kemper and Cole). I got a sudden sick feeling. Did Zach think he was going too die? Was he trying to say good-bye? I told him that I would tell them. I tried to reassure him that everything was going to be fine. I said that they were just going to go back in and try and stop some of the bleeding and that he would be back in a short time. As they were getting the permit ready for me to sign for him to

13

go back to surgery, Zach begin trying to tell me something. He motioned that he wanted to roll on his side and that he was hurting. The anesthesiologist was standing in the room and he said that his side was pretty torn up from being placed in that position all during the surgery. He thought it would be best if he did not turn that way. I asked if he could give Zach something else for pain or could he put him back to sleep. He said he would. I said can you just sort of keep him asleep the rest of the night? The anesthesiologist said he thought he would do that. I told Zach that he needed to just stay in that position and that they were going to give him something for pain. The anesthesiologist gave Zach some additional medication in his IV line. By the time I turned around from signing the permit Zach seemed to be asleep. His eyes were closed. I hated to say anything or touch him in case he was asleep. I did not want to wake him if he had gotten comfortable. I got ready to leave the room and sort of leaned out to touch the end of the bed but really did not touch him.

We went to the waiting room and found a spot to rest for the night. Dr. Hanley had said that he would come out and let us know when they were finished and Zach was back in the unit. Apparently I had dozed off on the couch when Johnny woke me and said that Dr. Hanley was walking down the hall. It was now about 1:00 am. Dr. Hanley said that it had been the right thing to do. He said that they had found the bleeder and had stopped the bleeding. He told us that they had cleaned out the lung area and Zach had done very well. Dr. Hanley said again that this was not a set back and that Zach was stable as a rock. We thanked him again and said that we hoped he could get some sleep. He told us that Zach would be back in the unit in a little while and then we could see him. I fell asleep again in the waiting room.

The Valley of the Shadow

I felt as if Zach was being pulled from me and I was trying to hold onto him with everything that was in me.

—Carla

"Dr. Hanley return to ICU stat!" blared over the intercom. I bolted off the couch and we both started running toward the unit. Johnny said, "Maybe it's not Zach." I said, "It has to be. He's the only patient Dr. Hanley has in this unit." When we got outside of the doors to the unit I had to stop. I thought I was going to faint. I told Johnny to go ahead and go see what was happening. He said, "I can't. I will just wait on you." We both were paralyzed with fear. We did not want to go in the unit even though we knew we had to. I finally was able to stand up and we walked to the desk. We asked the medical receptionist at the desk if it was Zach. She just nodded yes. She said that everyone was in there. That really is not a comfort since you know (well I know since I am a nurse) that it means that it is a code situation. We moved over to the side of the desk to wait.

Words cannot really describe what occurred over the next hour. I experienced the most intense physical struggle I have ever had in my entire life. I was begging God to stop the bleeding or whatever was happening in that room. I was begging God to save Zach. The physical, emotional, and spiritual war that seemed to be ragging in me was beyond description. I physically was overwhelmed by this powerful sensation that seemed to be pulling Zach away. I literally could not take a deep breath. I felt as if Zach was being pulled from me and I was trying to hold onto him with everything in me. At the same time I knew I could not physically survive what

15

I was feeling in my body. I was overwhelmed by a power more massive than anything I can describe. I fought for almost one hour. I finally released Zach. I felt like my spirit said ok God he is yours. At that moment I experienced the greatest release I have ever felt. I cannot say it was a good sensation but it was the most peaceful sensation after the intense battle of that hour. I looked up at Johnny and said, "He's gone." He asked, "How do you know? " I said, "I just do."

At some point during that hour I went into the restroom. I remember looking in the mirror and thinking, *so this is what you look like when your child is dying.* I could not really get my mind around what was happening. It seemed so surreal. Like a bad dream. Johnny went to call my parents at the hotel and tell them that they needed to come to the hospital. It was about three in the morning.

The nurse in charge finally came and told us that the surgeon would come out and talk to us in a few minutes. They took us to the consultation room. I knew that nothing "good" every happened in that room. We asked for my parents to be able to come back into the room with us but the nurse said that the surgeon wanted to speak with us alone at first.

We sat in the room and waited. We knew what we were going to hear but we sat there in a numb shock. The surgeon and the anesthesiologist walked into the room. They both looked terrible. Dr. Hanley sat down and he said, "I do not know what happened. Zach was fine. He should not have died." He went on, "I know that I cannot be as devastated as you all are but I am truly devastated." We asked at that point if my parents could join us. They said fine and I went to get them.

I walked out into the dark waiting room where other family members were trying to sleep. I looked at mom and dad and said, "He's gone." My mom fell against the wall screaming. My dad began to sob. Kemper who had come with my parents to California stood looking bewilder and crushed. I tried to gather them around but the shock and pain was so intense that they just stood where they were and cried.

Eventually, I was able to say that I wanted them to come in and hear what the surgeon had to say. They tried to compose themselves so we could go back inside.

When we went in again the surgeon said again that he did not know what had happened. He explained that the anesthesiologist had just been getting ready to leave for the night and Zach was doing great. He said all of a sudden the anesthesiologist heard a change on the monitor and looked up. When he did it showed that Zach did not have a heart beat or any blood pressure. He said that his blood pressure had been totally normal seconds before. Dr. Hanley said that they immediately started CPR and did effective CPR for one hour. They were never able to get a heart beat back. I asked if he had bled out from where the bleeding had been earlier. He said, "No." He said Zach was not bleeding at all. He was stable. I asked if he thought he had thrown a clot and Dr. Hanley said he did not think that had happened either.

Dr. Hanley said, "I hate to ask this but would you agree for us to do an autopsy so we can see what happened." I told him, "We will let you do an autopsy because I understand medically that you need to know what happened. But, I will tell you what happened. God just took Zach home." The doctors just looked at us.

I told Dr. Hanley that I hoped he would not doubt his ability or question what he had done. I told him what a blessing he had been to so many children. I knew that God had used him in so many children's lives.

The doctors expressed again their heart felt sorrow and ask what they could do for us. They suggested that we not see Zach. Dr. Hanley said that Zach was pretty bad looking after one hour of resuscitation. He thought we might not want to see him that way.

Johnny asked the doctors if we could pray. We stood and Johnny prayed the most beautiful prayer I have ever heard. He thanked God for the doctors and the talent He had given them. He thanked them for giving us hope if only for a moment. He asked God to bless them and the work they did. He thanked God for allowing us to know and be Zach's parents. He gave God glory and praise from a broken heart.

The doctors left and we were going to wait until they had cleaned Zach up and sent him to the morgue. Somehow I needed to see an empty bed in that unit so that I knew that I was not leaving him there. The nurse part of me thought that it might be wrong not to see Zach. Normally, seeing the body is part of the closure process but somehow it did not seem right to see Zach's body. I had seen a healing begin in Zach's physical body after he came back from surgery. I had seen him pink. Now he was completely whole and freed from his fragile body that had not been able to contain the bigness of his spirit. He was running now. He was not out of breath. He was home. I had lived in light of this moment for 18 years. The one time I had not expected Zach to die God took him home. All of the times man had said he would die he had not. When man said he would live, God chose to take him home.

The minutes, hours and days to come were some of the most painful I have ever experienced. God is faithful and carried us when we could not walk and held us when we could not stand. We planned on using the Caring Bridge website for a couple of days to let people know what had happened and about the memorial plans.

What occurred was beyond anything we had thought about. Johnny and I begin to post on the Caring Bridge website what we were thinking and feeling. People began to post responses to us. They asked us to keep writing because it helped them know how to pray and what was going on without having to bother us. To our amazement we found that it was helpful to pour out our feelings onto a blank page. We did not have to talk to or see anyone but we could share from the rawness of our hearts. It was a safe place to unload. The response was unbelievable. The remainder of the book is a collection of our journaling and others responses. Because this was "real" time journaling the many faces of grief are seen. The differences in Johnny's grief and my grief are evident.

Our hope is that you will see the real pain of grief but also the amazing furious love which God showed us. We also hope you will see the heart of a young warrior who trusted that God is in control and God is good.

Ultimate Healing

Zachary King Morton experienced the ultimate healing on December 5, 2003, and went to his true home to be with his Abba.

—Johnny

Friday, December 5, 2003 7:15 AM CST

Zachary King Morton experienced the ultimate healing on December 5, 2003, and went to his true home to be with his Abba. We know that Zach is where God created him to be for eternity. Zach's heart stopped at 2:30 am PST. The doctors performed CPR for an hour before giving up. Our last visits with Zach were very precious. He looked great! He was pink, not blue!

Zach was an incredible gift that God allowed all of us to share in for 18 years. He had more passion for life than anyone I ever knew. We know that we will grieve for him the rest of our lives, but we also must celebrate his life and the love he had for God and his family. His legacy lives on as we do that! Paul said that we do not grieve as those without hope. We know that we will be with Zach again and it will be awesome! Thank you for loving Zach the way that so many of you did. We will be forever grateful.

Still resting in Jesus!!!

Johnny, Carla, Kemper, Cole, and especially.........Zach!

I can name no other person in my lifetime, who can more confidently and truthfully claim to have fought the good fight, finished the race and kept the faith. Today Zach wears the crown of righteousness, given to him by the Lord God Himself. Wouldn't we all wish to have touched as many lives as Zach did in his 18 short years? Praise God for Zach Morton.

—Charlie Parrish

If anyone should hear the words "Well done my good and faithful servant", Zach, it's you. This place will never be the same without you here, but it will also never be the same BECAUSE you were here. Your love for our huge family and for God was evident in everything that you did and it is easy to see that by looking at all the lives you have effected. I have never and I'm sure I will never know anyone with the passion for life that you had. God knew exactly what he was doing when he put you on this Earth in the condition that you were in and he used that to touch so many lives and inspire so many people. I thank God that I got to be a part of your life, even if it was only for a short 18 years. Zach, you knew where you were going when you left this Earth and I know where you are. Until I see you again...I love you.

—Maggie

Johnny, Carla, and family
I saw Zach touch people's lives almost daily. When I first met Zach I could tell that he had struggles on a consistent basis, but he never let us "see" his pain. I could only imagine how often others in his situation would want to have everyone around them know how much pain and anguish they were in. Zach, however, did not let on. He fought the ultimate fight and won victoriously!!!

—Davey Keys "Chief"

Tuesday, December 9, 2003 7:37 PM CST
It seems ages ago that I posted the news of Zach's passing. These days have passed with agonizing slowness. At times the pain is so intense; we feel we cannot even breathe. But be assured that God's grace is covering us. We know the

20

prayers being lifted up for us are being answered.

I know tomorrow will be difficult for all of us. There is finality about laying Zach's body to rest even though we know Zach is not here. I say thanks in advance for the prayers that I know will be lifted up on our behalf.

Please pray that God's love and sovereignty will be magnified at the memorial service tomorrow. We want to celebrate Zach, but we also celebrate the God who made Zach so special to so many. Pray for David Jones, Zach's cardiologist, and me, as we will both be speaking at the service. We need God's strength and peace desperately. My prayer is that even in death; Zach will continue to impact the lives of others. Thanks again! Johnny

WEDNESDAY, December 10, 2003 8:38 AM CST
Please join us for:
A Memorial Service to Celebrate the Life of
Zachary King Morton
The Middlebrooks Athletic Center
First Presbyterian Day School, Macon Georgia
Wednesday, December 10, 2003 at 4:00pm

As you can imagine, my heart is full of pain as I write to you. Carla and I had known for years that Zach might leave us, but our imaginations never came close to the pain we feel. It is as if a very part of us is missing. I can see Zach in my mind, I can hear his voice and laughter, but when I want to hold him.... He's not there.

As deep as it is, our pain is tempered by the knowledge that Zach is experiencing a freedom and peace he never knew here on earth. Selfishly, we want him back, even for a little while. We thank God though that Zach will never have to struggle for a breath or face another doctor's visit again. He is with his Abba and knows face-to-face what the rest of us long to see.

One of the songs that makes me think of Zach whenever I hear it is Stephen Curtis Chapman's "The Fingerprints of God." As many of you have experienced personally and others have read in the many comments, Zach had the fingerprint of God all over him. He truly was one of the special people in this world and we feel blessed to be his parents!

After Zach died came the questions. Why here and now God? Why couldn't this happen closer to home? Why didn't you take Zach during the surgery when we might have expected something to go wrong? We had always said we would rather lose Zach during a surgery than to sit by and watch him slowly wither away. God answered that desire. I also believe God allowed Zach to make it through the surgery so we could have those last few precious minutes with him. His color looked great and we had a chance to express our love to Zach and he to us. What a great gift from God!! Being in California allowed us a day to grieve alone before returning home. And finally, the way Zach's heart just stopping seemed to be God's affirmation that He would decide when to take Zach home. Zach had run his race; he had finished the course; he had kept the faith, and all heaven cheered him home.

Well done Z-Man! Johnny

Wednesday, December 10, 2003 10:56 PM CST

We woke up to a gray, overcast sky with a forecast of thunderstorms. It was raining lightly as we made our way to the cemetery late this morning. As soon as Carla, the boys and I had sat down under the tent; Reverend Jerry Dingmore began the service with prayer. As he prayed, the heavens literally opened. It was an incredible display of God's power as seen in nature. The wind was so strong that the rain was blowing sideways. I remember looking out at my nephew standing outside the tent. He was holding his umbrella behind him instead of over his head because the rain was coming in sideways. I said a little thank you that the P.A. system was portable. I'm afraid Jerry may have been electrocuted if it wasn't. As soon as the service was winding down, the storm abated. Carla later said that it was as if God was sharing in our grief during the service. Heaven wept even as we were experiencing a supernatural calm as we laid Zach's body to rest.

We know for Zach death has no sting. There is no victo-

22

ry for the grave because Zach is running with you, Father. Since Zach was born, you have put us in a place where we had to trust in you completely. Keep us there even now! You are our peace. You are our joy! Everything we need is found in you. We love you, Abba! Johnny

Dear Carla & Johnny,

We came to the memorial service yesterday hoping to offer you and the boys some measure of comfort and support. We left knowing it was us who were comforted. Isn't that just like you! Johnny you did an amazing job speaking. God's grace shone through you in a mighty way. As I sat there listening to you, it reaffirmed that God's wisdom is perfect. He choose you both to be Zach's parents long ago, knowing all the while that you would have the grace, strength and faith to honor Him even in your darkest hours. If you can honor and serve Him so well even in the midst of your grief, how can I not do more to serve Him in my own life? I know that your words and the service will have a lasting impact on those who were there just as Zach's life will have a lasting impact on those who knew him. The surgeon was not completely wrong in saying that Zach was "stable as a rock." He was just mistaken in thinking he was describing Zach's heart when really he was describing his life.

—The Collins Family

Step-by-Step

We always said we did not want Zach to face a slow,
lingering death but the shock of him actually being gone
is too much to take in. Jesus tells us to store up our treasure
in heaven. We just deposited a major asset there.

—Johnny

Thursday, December 11, 2003 5:08 PM CST

Thank you God for your presence yesterday! We rested in your arms all day long as you carried us. Zach would have been in awe at all the people that came to the memorial service at FPD yesterday. Thank you for your presence, prayers, kind words, and tears. Your sharing in our grief is a great help!

Pray for our families as we struggle to get back to work and the other aspects of daily living. Our lives will never be the same again, but God does not call us to hide away from the world. We will continue to walk in God's grace day-by-day, step-by-step.

I know it will be difficult for our families in the days ahead. Everywhere we go we are reminded of Zach. I know that when you first see us you may wonder what to say. It is okay to talk about Zach! We can't forget him if we try. It is a comfort to know that you can't either. We have learned much about Zach as you have shared your memories with us. Please don't stop!

Resting in Him, Johnny

Friday, December 12, 2003 9:08 PM CST

It has been a week since Zach stepped into eternity. It is amazing how long a week can last. At times it seems only moments ago we were telling Zach goodbye as he left for sur-

24

gery. But then, it seems ages ago when I last held him or heard his voice. How I wish I could go back to that Wednesday before the surgery. I want to talk to Zach, to watch Sports Center together one more time, to tell him again how much I love him.

Grief is strange. It seems to always be changing. At first, the pain was so much we could not breathe. Then comes the numbness, as if you have no more tears to shed. You ask yourself "What is wrong with me? Why have the tears stopped?" And then, maybe a voice you hear or the face of a grieving friend and the tears come unbidden from wherever they have been hiding.

Everything else seems to lose its appeal. Things that just a week ago would have seemed wonderful are nothing right now. You know it has only been a week, but you wonder if anything will ever seem really joyful again. You can't imagine that it will. You find yourself in the midst of doing something and then wondering why? You look forward to sleep because you know the time seems to pass more quickly when you are sleeping.

They say that grieving the loss of a child is a process that can take years. I don't want to feel like this for so long. I find myself running to God more than ever. I need His words to give me hope and comfort. I want the joy that comes in the morning after a night of weeping! It does not say though how long the night lasts. I hope it is a short one.

Still in our Abba's arms,
Johnny & Carla

Sunday, December 14, 2003 0:09 AM CST
"Do not store up for yourselves treasures on earth, where moth and rust destroy, and where thieves break in and steal. But store up for yourselves treasures in heaven where moth and rust do not destroy, where thieves do not break in and steal. For where your treasure is there your heart will be also." Matthew 6:19-21

The whole thing still seems surreal. We have been through the funeral and memorial service, but the fact that

25

we will not see Zach again on this side of eternity just does not seem real. We are not playing a game of denial. We know Zach is gone. We miss him terribly. There is still expectancy though that he could walk in any minute. Maybe that is the mind's way of dealing with the shock? We always said we did not want Zach to face a slow, lingering death but the shock of him actually being gone is too much to take in. Jesus tells us to store up our treasure in heaven. We just deposited a major asset there. Believe me that our thoughts and desires will be more heavenward than they have ever been. Zach's passing has reminded us of our alien nature. Our citizenship is in heaven, not here! Activities and diversions that satisfied us in the past will never do so again. That's the way it should be. God tells us to live in light of eternity and let those things that will last be the source of our joy. Too often in the past, I have allowed those temporal things of this earth to be my focus. I pray that those things will continue to pale besides the reality of living in light of eternity. Thank you for your continued prayers. We know our strength must be renewed day by day!

Celebrating Life!

Johnny

Sunday, December 14, 2003 10:54 PM CST

"You shall know the truth and the truth will set you free."
John 8:32

I find myself clinging to that verse more and more. As numbness and wondering "what if?" seeks to overcome me, I find myself constantly in need of God's truth. These are some of the truths I find myself clinging to:

* God is sovereign. He is in absolute control.

* Receiving Zach to Himself was an act of incredible love.

* Even Zach's death will be worked out for my good. God will use it to make me more like Christ.

* There is still purpose to my life, even when I feel empty of purpose.

* God will continue to glorify Himself through Zach's death.

26

* God loves Zach more than Carla or I ever could.

* We were created for God's glory and to spend eternity with Him.

* This time and place where I now am is only temporary.

* Zach finally knows what it means to be fully human, something I can only imagine.

* We are in spiritual war and Satan will seek to keep God from receiving glory by Zach's life and death. I REFUSE TO LET SATAN WIN!

* God is my strength and refuge!

*God is sovereign! He is in absolute control!

Standing on the Truth! Johnny

Monday, December 15, 2003 4:28 PM CST

I haven't written anything since Zach went home. Words are very inadequate to explain grief. I am so amazed at how physical the grief is. There are days and moments that my body is so heavy it physically cannot move. The numbness is good but I know it cannot last. The feeling is like someone is sitting on your chest. It's like you can't catch your breath. I try to picture what Zach is doing and to know that as much as he loved me, he would not want to leave his new home. But, I am selfish and I miss him so. It struck me today when my cell phone went off that I would give anything for one more call from him. I know that Jesus will heal and restore us, but the hole is awful HUGE now. Thanks for your continued prayers. We know that is what is carrying us through these moments. Carla

Tuesday, December 16, 2003 10:34 PM CST

"But we do not want you to be uninformed... about those who are asleep, that you may not grieve, as do the rest who have no hope." I Thessalonians 4:13

I have read a lot about grief and losing a child in the last few days. You are told about the stages of grief and how important it is to go through them. Somehow that doesn't set right with me. There seems to be a path you must walk. My response: "Says who?"

27

I know that I have just begun a journey of grieving the loss of Zach and coming to grips with all that it means. I lost my firstborn son, my sports partner, my travel companion, my relief driver, my babysitter, my taxi when I need a ride, my news source, my "March Madness" cohort, most of my cellular bill, my football rival(War Eagle! or Go Dawgs!), my assistant coach, my sports rumor guru, my lunch partner, my confidant, my friend. There is an emptiness that I have never known.

But I still can't think of Zach as dead. He is more alive than he has ever been! This is what God created Zach for, eternity with Him. I was stepping out of the shower yesterday, half-way expecting to collide with Zach. (We shared a bathroom for showers.) I asked myself "when will you realize Zach is dead?" The Holy Spirit immediately brought to mind the passage about Mary seeking Jesus at the tomb. The angel asked her, "Why do you seek the living among the dead? He is not here." Luke 24: 5 that is how I feel about Zach. I can't grieve as if he is dead, because he is not! He is experiencing life free from sin and any physical or spiritual limitation.

I have always taught that a Christian's true home is in heaven. It is only when we get there that we will experience life as God intended it to be from the beginning. Do I abandon what I believe in the face of death? Now is the test of what I believe. As Max Lucado wrote, "If God is not God in death then He is not God at all." It is the promise of Christ that keeps me from grieving as one without hope. Christ is my hope and my promise that Zach is more alive now than ever!

Pray that our families will cling to God's promises and His truth. That is the key to grieving.

Resting in Him! Johnny

Thursday, December 18, 2003 11:06 AM CST

As I knew they would, the days continue to be an emotional roller coaster. School has allowed me to focus on something other than Zach, but at the same time, I am so aware of his absence when I am at school. I am grateful for

28

so many great memories of Zach at school.

Carla and I both mentioned that as we see people when we are out, there seems to be awkwardness. People do not seem to know what to say. Please feel free to talk about Zach. It is nice to know that he is missed. Your reminders that we are in your thoughts and prayers is also an encouragement and a comfort. I will admit though, it is sometimes hard to respond when someone asks, "How are you doing?" Right now we are just trying to get from day-to-day. There is sadness and a hole in our hearts that we long for Jesus to fill with His presence and comfort. We know that God is faithful to take care of us. Right now, we continue resting in His promises and truth.

Johnny

Sunday, December 21, 2003 2:00 AM CST

It's been 2 weeks since Zach died. It seems ages. The pain isn't as sharp as it was, but it has been replaced by a deep sadness. There is a loneliness there that I feel even in a room full of people. The memories of Zach are everywhere I go, but I want more than the memories. I want my cell phone to ring and hear Zach say "What's up?" when I answer. I wait up at night and wish he was coming in late so we could talk about the football or basketball game. I want him to come into my class at school and hear him ask, "Do I need to pick up Cole?" I want to rub his head right after he's had a haircut. I realize that I have lost more than a son; I have lost the best friend I had, next to Carla. Memories are sweet and I thank God that we have so many good ones, but they will never match up to the real thing. What I would give for one more day with Zach.

Clinging to Jesus,
Johnny

Sunday, December 21, 2003 11:48 PM CST

Carla and I were talking last night about all that has transpired over the past weeks. As we talked about Zach's life, we realized that Zach was who he was because of growing up with the struggles he had. His incredible character

29

was formed in the fires of suffering, and yet most people were never aware of his daily battles. Zach had an incredible gift to love people with no strings attached. Only in these past weeks have we even become aware of how many people Zach touched and with whom he had unique and vibrant relationships. Thank you for sharing with us these past weeks about how Zach touched your life. Johnny

Christmas with Jesus

*"I even I am He who comforts you." (Isaiah 51:12) I
keep reminding the Lord to "bring it on" since he promised.*

—Carla

Tuesday, December 23, 2003 7:47 AM CST

We had Christmas dinner with Carla's family last night.
Zach's absence was tangible. The pain for both of us was
almost as severe as those first hours after his passing. We
cannot ignore Zach's absence, but we want the other children to have a good Christmas.

A friend shared with me how he lost a sibling when he
was young. As he remembers it, all the fun his family used
to have disappeared after the death. We don't want that to
happen. What a disservice to Zach's legacy as he was so full
of fun and life. The pain of his absence is so intense right
now though. Please pray that God will fill us with an extra
measure of grace as we celebrate Jesus' and Zach's life
together this Christmas. Our hearts are so heavy right now
only He can fill them with joy!

Emmanuel! Johnny & Carla

Tuesday, December 23, 2003 12:21 AM CST

Zach loved Christmas. I know he liked presents, but it
was more about being with family. A friend gave me an orna-
ment that said "I'm spending my Christmas with Jesus!" I
will focus on that as we celebrate the season.

One thing I did realize yesterday is that Christmas takes
on a whole new depth to me now. I have always known what
the real reason for the season is but I do love all the presents
(the more the better) and family fun stuff. With all of that

31

empty and meaningless right now, I see what the gift truly meant. I did not willingly give up my son, but God did for me. I can know Him and be assured of being with Zach again because He gave us the gift. Love, Carla

Wednesday, December 24, 2003 2:29 PM CST
It is Christmas Eve and how I wish I could turn back the time. The heaviness of Zach's absence is overwhelming. Everything we do, everywhere we go, makes the loss feel like a hand squeezing our hearts. But we know that God's grace will sustain us.

Yesterday, Larry (Carla's Dad) and I went to the cemetery to meet with someone to help us with a headstone for Zach's grave. As Kitty had said the previous day, Zach isn't in the cemetery. I know his body is there awaiting Christ's return, but I have no memories to associate with that place and Zach. I am thankful for that. Being at home is another matter altogether.

This morning was heart wrenching. Before Zach died, he had bought a gift for Cole. He wanted to send it to him because he knew how excited Cole would be to get a package in the mail. Sadly, we never got to send it. Zach had also told me what to get Kemper and Cole for Christmas from him, if he did not get home in time to shop. We gave them both of these gifts today, not wanting to make Christmas day any harder. Zach had sent a note to Cole with his package. Typical of Zach, it was full of love and hope. I hope Cole will remember how much Zach loved him and how proud he was of his 7 year old little brother. I am afraid that with Cole being so young, He will only have vague recollections of his big brother. What a tragedy that would be! Please God! Don't let him forget!!!

Tonight and tomorrow will be a long day. Thank you God for the promise of your presence!
Hurting and Hoping,
Johnny & Carla

Thursday, December 25, 2003 0:47 AM CST

Dear God,

More than anyone else, you understand the pain of losing a son. You understand a father's love for his son and the agony of separation. How does God separate Himself? How did you forsake your own son willingly as He became my sin? I don't know how, but I do understand why. Because you are LOVE!

Thank you God for the gift of your son!

Thank you God for the gift of my three sons!

Thank you God for taking Zach home out of this world of sin, pain, and suffering.

Thank you God that my separation from Zach is only for a season.

Thank you God for 18 incredible years with Zach!

Thank you God for the legacy of love Zach left behind.

I love You, God!

Happy Birthday Jesus!

Celebrating His Son & mine,

Johnny

Friday, December 26, 2003 2:03 PM CST

I wanted to thank those of you who prayed for us yesterday. We could feel the prayers. The boys had a good day. As the day wore on it got harder to just pretend Zach wasn't there. It's the moments that you think about how long it might be before we see him that overwhelm the mind and heart. When you just think about the second you are in you can kind of pretend. But, then the reality of the loss of his presence from this life as long as it goes on, hits you. It's also so hard to think about years ahead when people will not remember and when there will be new memories without Zach in them. Johnny cried last night and said, "I don't want to make memories that he is not in." We know we will, and that's the way it is, but it's so hard. The verse in Isaiah 51:12 says, "I even I am He who comforts you." I keep reminding the Lord to "bring it on" since he promised. Cole got in the bed with me last night and put his arm around me and said, "I love you. Thanks for all of my presents. Merry Christmas."

33

I was so grateful to have him to cuddle with. Again, thanks for walking with us. Love Carla

Saturday, December 27, 2003 3:39 PM CST
It has been three weeks since Zach died. Most of the time his death still seems so unreal. As Carla said yesterday, it is the moments when you realize how long it may be until we see Zach again that are the most difficult. I will be 45 in a month. I cannot imagine living until 70 or 80 and not seeing Zach. We have learned to focus on the next hours, maybe the next day. I can only handle that.

My prayer and hope is that Zach's legacy will not be short-lived. I want his life to continue to make an impact in the lives of people here. It makes it easier if I can see God continue to change lives because of Zach and his life. Whether it be through teaching, writing, or speaking I want God to draw people to Himself through the testimony of Zach's life. Still celebrating!
Johnny & Carla

Monday, December 29, 2003 1:11 AM CST
It's about 2:15am here in Macon. You may have noticed that I post to this journal early in the morning. I find it hard to go to bed. For so many years I waited for Zach to come home before I would go to bed. I guess old habits die hard. I hate admitting that he's not coming home. There is still an air of expectancy. Any minute, I expect to hear the door open and see Zach walking in. I wonder how long that lasts.
Johnny & Carla

Monday, December 29, 2003 8:53 PM CST
"You shall know the truth, and the truth will set you free." John 8:32

Today was a hard day. I ordered the headstone for Zach's grave. It set me off down a road of melancholy. I began to question why we even let Zach have surgery. I cried; I screamed; I moved deeper and deeper into depression. As I began to wallow in self-pity, the Spirit came to my rescue with the verse above. What is truth? The truth is that God is in control as He always is. The truth is that Zach's days were numbered by God before Zach was even born. Part of God's divine plan for Zach's life was that He was going to take Zach home on December 5, 2003.

My faith in all that I have taught and believed has been tested these past days more than ever. Instead of running from God, I find myself seeking Him and His promises more than ever. I cannot make it without Him! He truly is my strength, my refuge, my comfort. The days ahead are sure to be difficult, but my Abba is ever faithful. He will sustain me. He shall turn my mourning into dancing. Amen!

Johnny

Forever Changed

I was thinking this morning about the saying that
"War is Hell." I think "Grieving is Hell."
It is this moving target that constantly changes.

—*Carla*

First and foremost, a part of our heart is forever gone.
The wound will heal and not be so sensitive in the years
ahead, but the missing part will never be replaced here on
earth. Yes we are still parents to two awesome boys, but
when Zach died, a part of us left this time and place with
him. We will one day be made whole, but not this side of eternity. You cannot lose a child and not be forever changed.

Secondly, our view of this life and what is important will
not be the same. This is a good thing as we begin to see the
value of things in light of eternity. The temporal things of this
world no longer can satisfy us. We want to know the satisfac-
tion that will only come when we are with Jesus and our family is reunited one day.

The pain that wrought these changes in us is more than
we could ever imagine. Nothing prepared us for that. I don't
believe anything could have. I pray that as we go through
this dark valley we will see the "peaceful fruits of righteousness" that God promises in Hebrews. May He be glorified
even in our pain!

Saturday, January 3, 2004 4:13 PM CST

Thank you for the encouragement you give us and especially for the stories of how God has used this site and Zach's
life to bring glory to the Kingdom. I am grateful that God continues to use Zach as a vessel of honor.

The grief feels like when you hurt a body part, maybe just

a finger, and no matter how hard you try to protect the wound, you end up banging it on everything in your path. No matter where we are or what we do, the memories of Zach hover around us. For both Carla and I sleepless nights are the norm. God's presence is felt, but the emptiness created by Zach's absence is always there.

This was one of Zach's favorite times of the year, school holidays and football overload! I had a hard time enjoying the games though. Even watching Georgia avoid a collapse was dampened by Zach's absence. I do hope he appreciated my rooting for Auburn! I know my mom missed him greatly today, too. Zach would always come over to watch Georgia. Tech with her whenever they played on TV. It reminds me that others miss Zach as we do. We thank Him for the blessing Caring Bridge has been to us.

Resting in His Arms, Johnny & Carla

Sunday, January 4, 2004 11:12 PM CST

I had a chance to watch a message on God's glory. It was a great reminder that all of life is about God and His glory. I reflected on how much Zach did just that; he was a reflection of God's glory. God allowed Zach to show us a glimpse of His unconditional love. When Zach's purpose was fulfilled, God honored him by bringing Zach home. He is a good God!

During these past days, God has continued to teach us and remind us of His goodness. I was thinking today of a family who lost their two children in a car accident the week before Christmas. I thought how tragic to suddenly and unexpectedly lose your only two children. I wondered if their parents have any regrets. Did they hug them before they left for school? When was the last time they had told their kids they loved them? Had they had a fight with the kids before they left for school? I thanked God that I had no regrets at all about Zach's death. God had taught us to enjoy each day with Zach and not take any for granted. For the most part we did just that. Even though the timing of Zach's death was unexpected, we had lived his whole life knowing that his life was in God's hands. We learned not to miss the opportunities God gave us. Because of that I can say that we have nothing to regret. God's timing even allowed us to share our love with Zach and him with us before his homecoming. He is a good God!

Not a day goes by that I don't tell Kemper and Cole that I love them. I try to make sure that Carla never goes to sleep without knowing how much I love her. It is because of Zach that we have learned to redeem the time God has given us and not miss out on what is most important.

Following Him, Johnny & Carla

Monday, January 5, 2004 5:54 PM CST

It's been a month today since Zach left us. In some ways, it seems like I have lived 100 years in the last month. It is absolutely unbelievable what grief does to your mind, body, and spirit. Most of the numb feeling (it's definitely a gift at the very beginning) is fading. Now comes the very changing face of grief. Yesterday was a pretty good day for me. Last night though was one of the worse nights. So, you just never know what each day will bring.

Last night I thought about how Zach always announced his arrival at home. He would start blowing his car horn when he got to the Slocomb's house next door. He would blow all the way up the hill and into the drive way. It was sort of his "calling card." I would always just smile and think how grateful I was that he was home. I was wondering what kind of announcement was made as Zach made his way to his eternal home. Do the others in heaven shout? Does Jesus cheer you through the door? I wonder if I'll ever get to know how it was when he arrived. Was Zach surprised that he was there? These are the sort of thoughts I've been having. Wanting him here but knowing that he really is at home.

Taking it a moment at a time, Carla

Wednesday, January 7, 2004 10:02 AM CST

I shared a devotional with my class this morning using First Thessalonians 4:13, "*We do not grieve as those without hope.*"

I talked about how one of the differences between Christianity and other beliefs is that we can have certainty about what happens after we die. It is the promise of eternal life as guaranteed by Christ that gives us the ability to grieve with hope. No other belief offers the certainty we find in Christ. At best, men are left to wish.

I also shared how my perspective on life has changed. I am learning to take each day for itself, to live each moment with purpose. The biggest change though is my perspective on eternity. I long for heaven. I understand as never before that "to die is gain!" I can't wait to get there! Thank God for the hope we have in Christ. Thank God that we can grieve knowing we will see Zach again. Death is painful, but the sting has been removed. Taking it one day at a time, Johnny

Wednesday, January 7, 2004 10:45 AM CST

I wanted to share one thing that made me laugh yesterday. You will have to bear with me to tell the story. I have only ventured out a few times. My mind is really not good enough to do more than that (those I work with will appreciate that). On Monday, I went to try and walk around the block and a dog ran out and bit me (it didn't hurt or break the skin) but it scared me. I thought, obviously this dog does not know that I am stressed and in grief.

The next day I went out to walk, (different direction). I stopped at the mail box to check the mail. The mail had not come but someone had put an envelope in the box. I just opened it to see who it was from and left it in the box. (It just had our first names, no address or a stamp so I thought it would be o.k.) You can probably guess what happened, the mail man came while I was walking and took the envelope. It might not have been a big deal but the envelope had a sweet note about wanting us to celebrate Zach and they had left cash for us to get a pizza. I jumped in the car (I had to go pick up Cole from school) and tried to find the mailman. I was already on empty on my gas tank, so this chasing the mailman did not help matters. I finally gave up and started to the gas station.

When I got to the station, a sign said "Pay inside First." I went to get my wallet and realized that I had taken it out that morning and left it on the kitchen counter. It had everything in it. I did not have any cash, credit card, check or a driver's license. I dug around and found $1.35 so I put less than one gallon in the car. It would not even make the light go off. (Thank heavens the sign was there about prepaying) otherwise I guess I would have been in Big trouble. I got to the school to get Cole and called Johnny. I said, "Please don't ask me how or why this happened but, I am going to run out of gas and I need you to get me." I knew what he was going to say. He said, "Can you not make it up the hill to the gas station?" I said, "No, I just spent my $1.35 and I cannot go back, I don't have anything." He told me to try to get to FPD, his school, and we would exchange cars.

I was telling Cole about what had happened as we drove. When we got to FPD, I was getting Cole out of the car and he said, "How come you didn't use my $20.00 bill?" I said, "I don't have your $20.00 bill." He said, "Yes, you do. My Chucky-Cheese wallet is in your pocket book." I looked and there was the "Chucky-Cheese" wallet right in my purse with a nice $20.00 bill. I started laughing so hard. I could not believe it. I thought how hard Zach would laugh. He had a great sense of humor and would laugh and laugh. He loved when I did "blonde things." I told Cole that Zach would have loved this one. I'm not certain that I'm going to leave the house today. I may not be safe. It was good to laugh, so I wanted to share it.

To end the mailman story, I was pulling into the neighborhood and behold there was the mailman pulling out. I flagged him down, jumped out and told him what happened. He was very nice and went through all the mail. Of course the letter was on the very bottom, but I did get it back. Again, thanks for caring.

One Moment at a Time, Carla

Friday, January 9, 2004 2:38 PM CST
We are struggling through each day. A family member gave me a CD she made with some beautiful songs. One of the lines is "Come and fill me with Hope because the climb is steep and the road is long." The day to day (minute by minute) climb is steep and the road looks long. I do not know

what we would do without the prayers. As Johnny wrote a day or so ago, he is struggling. School is very painful. He is not sleeping well and the grief is so painful.

Moment by Moment, Carla

Saturday, January 10, 2004 11:14 AM CST
I was thinking this morning about the saying that "War is Hell." I think "Grieving is Hell." It is this moving target that constantly changes. One moment you are hit with the reality that Zach is gone and it's so overwhelming. The next minute you feel just flat, like you're here but not really. Then you may have a moment that you do something that feels more "normal." You are back at overwhelmed before you know it. It just changes by the minute. Sometimes you feel hungry, like you want to eat. Other times the thought of food is revolting. Sleep is the same way. At times it is a sweet release and escape. Other times it is torture because you can't sleep. The body does amazing things (well really not amazing) in the midst of this kind of stress. You just cling to Jesus and ask Him to hold you and carry you. We know that God will bring the healing but it seems, most of the time, He uses the passage of time to accomplish it. We are touched by every act of kindness that has been shown to us. It is a sweet fragrance along this painful path.

Moment by Moment, Carla & Johnny

41

A Living Testimony

"I raised you up for this very purpose, that I might display My power in you and that My Name might be proclaimed in all the earth." Romans 9:17

—God

Sunday, January 11, 2004 8:02 AM CST
"We loved you so much that we were delighted to share with you not only the gospel of God but our lives as well, because you had become so dear to us." 1 Thessalonians 2:8

We were sharing with friends some of the stories people had shared with us about Zach over the past weeks, someone remarked about the way that Zach gave himself away to so many. That is so true. Zach's impact and legacy for a life so short was so great because Zach practiced what Paul talked about in Thessalonians. Zach was a living testimony to the love of God and he evidenced that by giving of himself. What a challenge my son's life has become to me!

As Carla posted yesterday, grief is a moment by moment thing. You never can tell what might hit you a certain way so that floods of pain, sadness, and sometimes even joy wash over you. Notes and cards are encouraging. Food is such a gift as the desire to plan and cook a meal at the end of the day is so often more than you want to tackle. Celebrating Life in Jesus! Johnny & Carla

Monday, January 12, 2004 4:39 PM CST
This has been a really bad day. It's like everyone is maybe being "oppressed." I had a hard time with Cole this morning. (He is having a hard time and just expressing it in different ways). Johnny did not sleep all night and tried to go to school

42

but came home sick. He is in the bed sick. He looks terrible (don't tell him I said that part). I don't know if all of the sleepless nights have caught up with him or if he has a bug. Reminding Jesus that He must carry us, Carla

Tuesday, January 13, 2004 11:27 AM CST
I have slept for about 20 of the last 24 hours. I think that is more than I had slept in the previous 5 days combined. I feel much better. I pray that God will allow me to sleep in a more normal pattern in the days ahead.

We have sought to honor God these past weeks and to allow Him to use us as vessels of His grace and sovereignty. I also know that such activity does not go unnoticed by the enemy. Thank you all for the hedge of prayer that has been put up around us. I believe that as God continues to use Zach's life and story to change lives that we will need that hedge continually. Standing against the enemy!
Johnny & Carla

Wednesday, January 14, 2004 8:27 PM CST
We have lived another day and consider it a victory. More than ever we are learning to walk day-by-day and allow God to carry us for that day alone. We have learned that to look too far ahead brings the pain of knowing Zach won't be there. I have found that thinking ahead and knowing Zach will not be a part of those future events is more painful than remembering the past. I know there will come a day when we can joyfully anticipate coming events, but it is much too soon for that. Wrapped in His arms!
Johnny & Carla

Friday, January 16, 2004 11:45 AM CST
It is now 12:50pm on Friday, January 16th. It has been six weeks since Zach died and at times it still seems unreal. His memory still pervades everything I do. On the way to school this morning, I heard a song by Aaron Tippin. Tears flooded my eyes as I remembered our trip to Washington, DC last year when we all sat under the Washington Monument and listened to Aaron Tippin in concert. I wish I could relive

43

that moment when our family was whole. I still can't believe he is gone!

Don't let me be so looking forward to heaven that I miss my opportunities here on earth. Thank you, LORD that I can look forward to seeing Zach again and know that we will never be separated again. Do hurry and come for us soon, though!

Day by Day, Johnny

Sunday, January 18, 2004 1:01 AM CST

A few days after Zach's funeral, Cole asked Carla how she knew Zach was in heaven. Carla went over the plan of salvation and God's promise to take us to heaven when we died. As they lay in bed, Cole gave his life to Christ. What a bittersweet moment; that God used Zach's death to bring Cole to Christ. What a joy to know that someday our whole family will spend eternity together!

I have received several letters from students whose lives have been changed as a result of Zach's death and the way God's grace has been so evident during this time. We have heard of families that started going to church again after following Zach's story on this website. Relationships between parents and their children have been renewed and strengthened. And finally, I received a call the other night from a man who had known Zach from the baseball park. He said he had to call me and tell me what an impact Zach had made on him. He shared how since Zach's memorial service God has shown him that he needs to give his life to Christ. Even after his death, Zach continues to point people to Christ. Thank you, God for your faithfulness to your promises. Thank you for bringing good out of what has been the most difficult time of our lives.

Celebrating God's Faithfulness! Johnny & Carla

Sunday, January 18, 2004 9:02 PM CST

Today was a really hard day for me. Today someone said to me, "Are you doing o.k. now?" I wanted to say," No, I'm not." Would you be o.k. in six weeks if your child died? I know they mean well, but it hurts to even think I could be

44

o.k. after losing part of myself. I have not felt as heavy or cried as hard as I have today since Zach died. I have struggled all day to try and make sense with my small little mind how and why this all worked out this way. The more I tried to get it in the "box" the more overwhelmed I felt. I curled up in my bed (many of you know how I love my bed) and told Johnny that I wished I could just stay right there. I told God, "I can't and don't want to try and figure any more. I just want to rest. All I know is that you get to be God, and I don't." That's about where I am today.

Moment by Moment, Carla

Wednesday, January 21, 2004 5:49 AM CST

Teaching at school is so hard. As I watched the students throughout the day, all I can think about is "Zach's not here." I do the things I have to do, but there is little joy or excitement right now. It reminds me of a time I had broken my ankle and torn the ligaments. I had been teaching a Bible study at a nearby state park. I injured myself down by a river. It didn't hurt so badly until I had to walk out of there. Every step I took was excruciatingly painful, but I did it because I had to. Now, I do those things I have to do, painful as it may be, because I have to. When I had broken my ankle, someone finally had to carry me out. Even now, I can only go on because Jesus carries me day-by-day, step-by-step.

Resting in Jesus arms, Johnny

Wednesday, January 21, 2004 9:22 PM CST

Romans 9:17 God says, *"I raised you up for this very purpose, that I might display my power in you and that my name might be proclaimed in all the earth."* That summarizes what God has been teaching me these past weeks. Everything in life or death is about God and His glory. He loves us and even sent Jesus to die for us, but even that was so God might be glorified. God's sovereignty in our lives was reinforced as we received the autopsy from Zach's death. Medically, they could find no physical reason that Zach's heart stopped. Kemper had said the day Zach died that they would not find anything in the autopsy. He was right. Zach's days were

45

numbered by God and he allowed Zach to die in a way that would show God's control. If it had been up to me, I would have let Zach live and continue to glorify God by his life, but it is about God, not me.

Johnny

Friday, January 23, 2004 10:48 AM CST

"All these people were still living by faith when they died. They did not receive the things promised; they only saw them and welcomed them from a distance. And they admitted that they were aliens and strangers on earth. People who say such things show that they are looking for a country of their own. If they had been thinking of the country they had left, they would have had opportunity to return. Instead, they were longing for a better country—a heavenly one. Therefore God is not ashamed to be called their God, for he has prepared a city for them." Hebrews 11:13-16.

More and more each day, I realize how much Zach's death has impacted my life. I am not the same person I was before. I have changed, and as Zach's life verse, Romans 8:28, proclaims, the change will be for good. Carla and I have both mentioned how things that brought joy before the events of the past weeks no longer do so. We realize that the things on earth will not satisfy. God has created in us a powerful heavenward vision. As I teach my students, I find myself feeling alien to this world I live in. That is God's plan. He doesn't want us to be satisfied here. This is not our home. We are created for eternity. Zach is truly home! I can't wait to join him.

Looking forward, Johnny

Jesus Carry Me Today

*Grief is like having a broken leg and trying to tell yourself
to just pretend or act like it isn't. You can't do it.*

—Carla

Friday, January 23, 2004 11:02 AM CST

I went back to work today. Being back in a familiar place
felt nice on the one hand, on the other hand it is like you're
trying to leave your grief behind and go back to "normal."
Even though I know I'm not leaving my grief, it seems like
your doing a disservice to your loved one. I know in my head
that it is part of the process to feel guilty about having
moments of "normalcy" but it feels very strange. It's very
mixed emotions. Well, really like the whole process is. You
feel a host of different emotions all at the same time. Part of
the challenge is to feel everything (which we must) but not to
get stuck anywhere. It's such a moment by moment process.

Moment by Moment, Carla

Saturday, January 24, 2004 11:12 PM CST

It is now been seven weeks since Zach went home. Our
grieving has manifested itself in so many various ways. I
seemed to have moved into a different stage. For the past
weeks there was always an air of expectancy that I had. My
cell phone would ring, and just for a moment, I'd think it was
Zach. Someone called about 11:00 p.m. one night and my
first thought was "Why are you calling this late Zach." As I
was getting ready for school, I'd find myself thinking I ought
to get Zach up. (He was a hard sleeper!) Ever since his death,
I kept expecting to hear him, see him walk in my class, hear
him blow his car horn, answer the phone and hear Zach say

47

"What's up?" Today, for the first time, I realized that air of expectancy was gone. I miss it though. I suppose the reality is setting in.

While the expectancy may be gone, the grieving goes on. I find myself avoiding situations that bring pain. When I am at a school basketball game, I don't look at the bench. He always kept stats and sat on the end of the row. I change the radio station when a song that reminds me of Zach comes on. I still find it hard to get to sleep, even just to get to bed. To go to bed when he has not come home is so hard. It is so painful to admit that he isn't coming home. I know that all of our memories of Zach are going to be a joy and comfort someday. Right now it is still so raw. I miss him so much!

Pressing onward, Johnny

Tuesday, January 27, 2004 7:30 AM CST

The song running through my head this morning has no great spiritual value, but it fits my mood today: *It's My Party and I'll Cry if I Want To.* It is my birthday today and I don't think I have felt this heavy and sad since the first weeks after Zach's death. I was not sure I could even get to school this morning. I have always enjoyed my birthdays, not minding Carla's teasing about how old I was getting. Today I feel incredibly old. I guess it flows from the adage "fathers shouldn't have to bury their sons." The loss of Zach from my life is so painful today. Jesus, carry me today! I can't do it without you!

Johnny

Wednesday, January 28, 2004 10:00 PM CST

As we have both said before, Carla and I continue to live day by day, trusting God to carry us each step of the way. You never know what may transpire as you begin each new morning. Yesterday was an oppressively sad day for me. Today was as good a day as I have had since Zach's death.

Even as I miss Zach, God reminded me that Zach is so much better now. I was searching our storage shed when I ran across an old pair of baseball shoes. They were in great condition, as if they had never been played in. It took me a minute to realize that they were Zach's. They never had been played in. I thought to myself how hard it must have been for Zach to have loved sports as he did and yet, never get to play. I remembered that he had bought the cleats to wear as he helped me coach Kemper's and Cole's teams. Zach so wanted to be a part of the game, even to the point of buying shoes he would never wear in a game. My heart ached. I thanked God for taking Zach home and freeing him from a body that kept him from the sports he so loved. I cannot wait until I get to heaven. After I see Jesus, I think I'll ask Zach if he wants to play some ball. How awesome will that be!

Giving Thanks! Johnny

Thursday, January 29, 2004 3:41 PM CST

Each day is truly a new adventure in this journey. It is really hard to find words to describe how it feels. Last night Cole came into our bedroom sometime in the middle of the night. Immediately when he entered the room, even though he was quiet, I was aware that he was there. He came in to tell me that he needed to go to the bathroom. When he finished he came back and said, "Now I'm going back to my room." He has a bathroom off of his room. I guess he just wanted to keep me "updated." I thought about how God must instill in Mom's that sense about the presence of their child. Ask any new Mom and she will probably tell you that she hears her new baby almost about the time they breathe hard or turn over. Not always, but most of the time Dad has to be nudged awake. I thought about the hour that Zach had died. We did not know he had died, but I knew he was being pulled from me. It was the most strange and unusual experience I have ever had. It is amazing how God really does make a child a "part" of you. Losing one is like losing part of you. Moment by Moment

Carla

Saturday, January 31, 2004 4:53 PM CST

Today was another really hard day for me. It's hard to explain how one day you can be fairly functional and another day you're just too heavy. I have been just "heavy" most of today. It's like you are emotionally flat. I realized that maybe after being out in the world for a couple of days I am just emotionally spent. It's not particularly what someone says or doesn't say. It's just having to keep your emotions in check and having to respond at all. I think after a couple of days of doing that I am wiped out. Thursday when I was at work they called a "Code." I knew it would happen; unfortunately in a large hospital it happens a lot. I was little shaken up when I heard the Code called. When Zach was dying, I was so afraid that they would call a code and then I would remember hearing that forever. They did not call a Code for Zach because the doctors were already in his room when his heart stopped. When I heard the code called at work I was immediately back in that unit awaiting word on what was happening with Zach. It was really hard. I wonder if I will do that forever.

When Zach was sent to Atlanta after his birth, he went in an ambulance with the siren on and the gas to the floor. When Cole was born 10 years later he was also sent to Atlanta via an ambulance with the siren on. Unfortunately, I left the hospital at about the same time and saw and heard the ambulance going up the interstate. To this day when I hear an ambulance, I am transported back to both Zach & Cole being in an ambulance when they were first born. The code situation may be like this for me also. Praying to be carried through another day, Carla

Wednesday, March 17, 2004 3:53 PM CST
I heard something on grief. They said how someone may look the same on the outside, but they are not the same on the inside. How true it is. I guess in a way when people see me dressed, out at work, doing whatever; it looks like I'm ok. In a way it's true. I am ok to the point that I was able to get dressed and drive the car. I realize some of you are concerned about both the above points, but never the less it "looks" normal. The reality is that it is not normal. At moments I find that I "feel" like maybe myself (but it is just fleeting). I quickly realize that I am not the same. The "old" myself has been so altered that I probably will not find that again. In some

50

ways it's probably good. But, in so many ways it is so strange to realize that I have been altered on the inside. The outside may look normal but the inside is not.

I told Johnny last night, "I don't know what will be worse to 'feel' the way we do now or to realize in years to come that we don't miss him as acutely." Both sides of the coin are bittersweet. I don't want to not miss him terribly, but I also don't like this surreal fog I'm living in. It's almost a scary feeling as each day we get further way from when he was here. I realize that it means we are one day closer to seeing him but that is hard to get my mind around. Unfortunately, what I know is the here and now. At moments it is still so unreal that Zach is gone. Hanging On, Carla

Wednesday, March 31, 2004 2:29 PM CST
It's so hard because "something" just seems not right. It's like your missing something. The day brought tears of joy mixed with tears of personal sadness and loss.

Life goes on. We must go on but it is so hard. It's so easy to get angry that other people's lives are not affected. They get to go on. Our lives are forever changed. At moments, I am angry. I wish it was different. Why us?

It is so hard to stay on top of the emotional rollercoaster. One minute you feel like being open and maybe talking or sharing. The next minute you feel like you have closed up like a clam. I feel annoyed. I get frustrated at how difficult it is to just "live." You can't plan, you can't "excel" because you're just surviving. At times I tell myself just "focus." But, it doesn't work that way. Grief is like having a broken leg and trying to tell yourself to just pretend or act like it isn't. You can't do it.

I think this grief is moving at a snail's pace yet at times I want to cling to the last thing I have of Zach, which is my grief.

Weary, Carla

Broken Hearts

I know we will spend eternity with Zach, but I will so miss sharing in his life during our days on earth.
                                                          —Johnny

Wednesday, February 4, 2004 10:17 AM CST

I continue to be amazed at this journey of grief. It has so many different faces. The last 4 days have been very heavy for me. It's like the heaviness is pervasive. It's not one particular thing it is just this overwhelming heavy, flat feeling. It is still so physical. Nothing tastes right. My coffee is not right (that's a major problem!). My body seems to keep responding to this grief in ways that let me know it's not "okay."

I was driving home from work and found myself saying out loud, "I can't believe it happened this way. I can't believe Zach is gone." At times, it is just so unreal. At moments I feel completely overwhelmed with the thought of not seeing Zach again in this life. It just seems unbearable. I miss him so. He was such a joy to me. He taught me so much about life. God used Zach to really mold me into the person I have become.

I started reading a book last night by a minister whose son was killed at 17 years of age. One of the statements he made in the book was, "The evening of death brings its own shadows, casting long ribbons of darkness and numbing every fiber of life. That darkness etched my soul in ways I never dreamed possible." In *Sit Down God I'm Angry* by R. F. Smith Jr. I so identify with his statement. In all my imaginings of losing Zach one day, it never came close to the reality of the loss and the power of grief. Believing that God is holding me even when I do not feel it,

Carla

"Believing that God is holding me even when I do not feel it." Carla thanks for reminding us what real faith looks like.
—Jerry Dingmore

Thursday, February 5, 2004 10:23 PM CST

Someone once said that when we lose a parent, we grieve the past that we shared with them. But, when we lose a child, we grieve all of the future we will never share with them. Having lost both my dad and my oldest son I can tell that the latter is far worse. I miss my father, but the memories had already been made, the special moments had been celebrated. With Zach, the 18 years seem but a moment. We had so looked forward to Zach finishing his senior year, Prom, Graduation, heading off to Auburn, all that we dreamed of sharing with Zach will not be. I dread the pain that I know will be there as we watch other parents and their children fulfill the dreams they had.

My sister-in-law, Pat, wrote a letter telling about Zach. She so eloquently captured our feeling of loss that I wanted to share some of her words:

"...Zach will never hit a home run, graduate from high school or college. He'll never meet and fall in love with the young woman of his dreams, who would agree to spend the rest of her life with him. He will never know the joys of fatherhood. He won't be the baseball coach, he dreamed of becoming. And he won't be at his brothers' graduations or weddings........."

I know we will spend eternity with Zach, but I will so miss sharing in his life during our days on earth. Tomorrow night is Senior Night for FPD basketball. During the ceremony, we would have walked onto the court to meet Zach. He would have given Carla a kiss and a rose. I so wish that would happen, but I know it won't, and we will grieve. Clinging to my Abba,

Johnny

Friday, February 6, 2004 10:56 PM CST

Bittersweet, that's what I told Kemper today would be as we drove to school this morning. My expectations were met

53

and then some. It was a hard day anticipating Carla and I going to the basketball game tonight. I knew it would be sad watching all the seniors be honored tonight, see them walk across the court, and know that Zach would not. Before they announced the seniors, Greg Moore, the school's Athletic Director gave a moving tribute to Zach followed by a moment of silence in his honor. It was a powerful and yet tender moment and I was so proud that Zach was my son. As tears welled up in my eyes I thanked God for the privilege of being Zach's father.

One of my fears in the early days after Zach's death was that while we would miss Zach terribly, others might not. I thought maybe people will share in our grief the first few days and then go on with their lives as usual. Nothing could be further from the truth. Two of Zach's classmates brought me a sweet card and a rose to give to Carla. All of these things and, even more, continue to affirm to us how awesome God's love is. Thank you God and thanks to all of you who continue to be God's instruments to demonstrate that love to our family.

Celebrating God's Son and mine,
Johnny

Dear Johnny and Carla,

I have been thinking about Zach and his absolute love for this time of year and how much I loved to sit and chat with him at the basketball games—as I told you before—he made this old teacher feel so terrific when he would come over to see me at games. He was a gift from God in my life to be who he was—no one else can fill Zach's place for me. He had such a zest for life and he always made me feel better when I was around him—what a gift! I can't possibly know the pain you feel, but I do love you both and know that the place of greatest darkness is the place in which our Father comes and covers us with His wings and whispers the most tender secrets of His heart to his precious overwhelmed, overcome, helpless, broken children.

You will hear His voice with greater clarity and certainty that He is saying, "This is the way—walk in it." The signifi-

cance of Zach's life and your lives (Johnny and Carla) in min-
istry will begin to unfold as you stay in this Secret Place of the
Most High God (Ps. 91). Out of such incredible grief, an incred-
ible joy will be birthed. God will be praised with greater meas-
ure than He has been thus far. The life in the Spirit, abiding,
seeking His leading, and obeying Him is the most exciting life.
The eternal becomes more real than the temporal. Learning to
hear His voice and know His heart will transform us forever in
what we do with our time and for our time. Please know I write
this with tremendous respect and humility and love for you. I
do miss Zach- I'd love for him to be my teacher and guide
when I get Home! Much joining with the hosts of saints hold-
ing you up before the throne,

—Gwen Weston

Tuesday, February 10, 2004 8:37 AM CST

It is just amazing how physical grief can be. Johnny said
yesterday that he read something on grief and it said you
should not try to do anything else the first year except just
daily routine things. The physical part of grieving is so con-
suming that it takes all of the energy you have. We are really experiencing this; just day to day living saps all of your
resources. Carla

Tuesday, February 10, 2004 8:47 PM CST

I have been sick the past couple of days. I know that
grieving takes a physical toll on your body. I have been sick
more the past 8 weeks than I have been the previous three
years. I am going to an oral surgeon tomorrow to have an
abscessed tooth removed. Sounds like fun doesn't it?

As I was preparing supper for the boys tonight, I realized
that I was getting used to Zach's absence and I hated it. I felt
guilty. I know that it is a defense mechanism our mind takes
to give us rest from the toil of grieving. I immediately began
thinking about my last days with Zach. Riding on the train;
eating at Nola's in New Orleans, Thanksgiving dinner at
Subway. As I remembered, the tears began to flow. The pain
was welcome as I felt Zach's absence as I had in the previous
weeks. In a strange way, the pain and sense of Zach not

being here makes me feel closer to him. Strange I know. Embracing the pain,
Johnny

Wednesday, February 11, 2004 10:29 PM CST
In my class today, I was discussing the concept of being spiritually dead to God. By way of illustration, I talked about various aspects of physical death. Later as I reflected on the day's lesson, I was surprised that I was not more emotional talking about death. I realized it's because I don't think of Zach as being dead. He is somewhere else right now where I can't get to him. I miss him and I long to hold him, but I don't think of him as dead. I believe that is part of what Paul was talking about to the Thessalonians. A Christian's grief is different because we know the one we grieve is not dead. How the world faces death with uncertainty or with the idea that death is the end, I don't know! I thank God for the promise of life in Jesus!
Celebrating Life!
Johnny

Friday, February 13, 2004 7:46 AM CST
I'm still so amazed at this grief process. I realized yesterday why I think you stay fatigued all of the time. It's like your mind, emotion, spirit and body are constantly processing. I realized that within an hour's time I can run a full range of emotions.

One minute I am thinking about Zach and how I can't believe he is gone. The next minute may be a thought about how long this grief will last. Then I find myself thinking that I don't want the grief to leave. The grief is my last connection to Zach. My memories will be there, but grief is the last emotional tie to him. Then I find that I feel so empty, like there's a big hole. Even if I'm not thinking about Zach, it's like something is missing. I may just be doing whatever but it's like my mind and emotions are in two different places. No wonder grief is so exhausting. I find that I am so tired at the end of the day even if I haven't done any thing. It is unbelievable how much energy it takes to get through the day.

My body continues to remind me that "something" is not right. Again, even when I am not consciously thinking about it, my body seems to know. I have had more stomach aches in the last 10 weeks than all of my life put together. It's like my body "knows" and reminds me. No wonder they say to just live is about all you can do at first.

Last night I read something about when we mourn. It said, "If you cannot mourn what was, then mourn what will not be." It reminded me that I have mourned all my life for Zach and his losses, now also for the loss of the future. I grieved and mourned when he was born with a severe congenital heart defect. I grieved all of the normal things I missed with a new baby.

I grieved his slow development. I grieved when I watched him struggle to stand up and then much later try to walk. I grieved each time he was left out at school or made fun of because he could not run. I grieved when he was left out of most kid's things, because he was not able to keep up. I grieved when he was not included or invited to be a part of the "group." I grieved when he would get frustrated and cry and scream and say, "Nobody understands what it is like to live like this. I can't do any of the things I want to do. It's so hard."

I sound kind of angry don't I? (Maybe I'm moving into the next phase). I know I need to remember all that we grieved over. But, I also know that Zach was an amazing rare gift. His life was very hard. For any parent to watch a child suffer and not be able to intervene is painful. To know Zach suffered most of his life is tough to do as his mom. To remember what he could have become and yet did not is a precious gift. To look back with awe at how he decided to get up every day and greet life is a gift. He choose to live fully the life he was given. For that I am grateful.

I miss him so. He was such a bright light in our lives. I wish I could just peek at him. I know he is doing wonderful, but oh how I want to check on him.

Trying to hold on in the dark,
Carla

Saturday, February 14, 2004 12:38 AM CST

The weather today matches my emotions. It is cold, damp, and raining. It's Valentine's Day. I so wish I could say, "I love you" to Zach. He would say, "I love you too." He was so free with his love and his hugs. I wish for one more hug.

Zach was always doing kind things on holidays. Last year he wrote me a sweet note and gave me money to buy a coke and a candy bar. I have the note in my billfold. He would have said or done something today for me.

I know it is the way it has to be, but, oh, the heaviness of our loss. Johnny said to me this morning, "I give you my heart even though it's broken."

Asking for strength and grace for the moment,
Carla

Saturday, February 14, 2004 11:32 PM CST

If ever a day was made for Zach, it was Valentine's Day, a day to express love to the special people in your life. Zach was all about loving people. From the time he was little, Zach showed a great need for people. He so wanted to be loved and he found that need met as he loved other people. He learned at a young age that the way to get love was to give it away unconditionally. Zach's whole life was built around his relationships with the people he loved.

I was reminded again today about those relationships. The relationships Zach had with the rest of our families were beyond the normal. Kathy, Carla's sister, remarked about the pain of losing Zach, "I'll never have a nephew that loved me the way Zach did." He had a special relationship with Kitty & Larry that went beyond a grandparent and grandchild. King, Carla's brother, was Zach's hero and mentor. To my Mom, he was her greatest joy after my Father passed away. There are others that still grieve every day as we do. My sister Jeanne reminded us today of how the grief and pain catches you unexpectedly. The times she's at church or Kroger and realizes Zach won't be sneaking up on her or giving his familiar high-five. Seeing him pulling up in his convertible. (It used to be hers.) Hearing his laugh at Sunday night pizza and especially his phone calls. I realized Zach belonged to many more people than just Carla and me. His capacity to love was so great and my grief is heavier tonight as I expand it from myself to grieve for the other parts of my family that have a broken heart on this day of celebrating love. Remembering a son, a grandson, a nephew, a cousin, and so much more!

Johnny

Monday, February 16, 2004 5:04 PM CST

Thanks so much for those who thought that this weekend might be hard and did extra things for us.

We had some precious, wonderful friends treat us to a night out of town. It was great. It was a little "reprieve" in this night of grief. You always carry the grief with you but some times just dropping out of life for a day really helps.

Right now we struggle just to get through the day. Just to hang on and really not lose our mind. At moments the whole thing is so overwhelming, I think I will not make it.

Still hanging,

Carla

One Step Forward, Two Steps Back

Everyday is grieving in triple....
I grieve what I lost.... I grieve the moment he is not in....
I grieve the future we do not have.

—*Carla*

Tuesday, February 17, 2004 5:31 PM CST

Today I helped the boys get ready for baseball. I was throwing in the yard with them. (Scary thought) I could not get out of my mind what Zach had said to the surgeon, Dr. Hanley. He had said, "I just want to be able to play ball in the yard with my brothers." I so thought this might be the spring. I thought he might get to do just that.

I know it was not to be, but I just can't seem to let it go. He would have had such a good time this afternoon. At times it is still so unreal. I guess it is like I mentioned before, everyday is grieving in triple. I grieve what I lost. I grieve the moment he is not in. I grieve the future we do not have.

It is all I can do to just stay in the moment. If I think at all too far ahead, I cannot stand it. I see now what it is to really be & live in the moment. That's all the strength I am given. If I look too much ahead, I am overcome. I get just what I need for that moment.

Moment by Moment,
Carla

Thursday, February 19, 2004 9:34 AM CST

I have been so heavy the last two days. I told someone that by the time I get to work I am exhausted. It's like there is just nothing to go on. Sadness and crying I would have expected, but this sensation is strange and foreign to me.

I thought last night about how we talk about not putting

stock in our feelings. How feeling can be misleading, even untrue. But I realized how we (or I) love to have "feelings." I want to "feel" God's presence. I want to "feel" something. I want God to show himself to me in a powerful way. And yet I find that I just have to trust that everything God says He is, and has promised is true. I do not feel it but I must believe it.

My night of grief is very dark. I know who is on the other side of the tunnel but it "feels" dark in here right now.

Believing He is holding me even when it doesn't feel like it. Carla

Friday, February 20, 2004 8:33 AM CST

Driving home last night there was a song that said, "Closer every day." It was talking about being one day closer to heaven every day. I was thinking about it. Then I realized that the truth is that I don't want to be one day closer to heaven and Zach. I want Zach here.

That sounds terrible, I am certain, but it is the way I feel. I want to hear Zach's voice call me on the phone, several times a day. I want to hear him say, "What's up?" Zach would always ask what I was doing. Then he would say, "What are we doing tonight?" He loved to know the plan and he loved to have plans. He would have the top down on his car today. He would be thrilled that it is going to be 70 degrees. He would be so excited about Region Basketball. He would be looking forward to baseball starting at the ball park.

I want him to help me with Cole. I miss him picking up Cole for me. I miss him running errands. I want to talk with him. I want to go get ice cream with him (his treat).

I wanted to see him graduate. I wanted him to get to have the 2nd surgery and get better. I wanted him to get to go to Auburn this fall. I wanted to go visit on a football weekend.

I wanted to see what God would do with his life. I wanted him here. It was not to be, but that's what I wanted. Zach's better off, but I am not.

Hanging moment by moment,
Carla

Saturday, February 21, 2004 11:45 PM CST

One step forward, two steps back. In this dance of grief, those are the steps we seem to be dancing. Since last Saturday, it seems the pain of Zach's loss is as fresh as ever. I thought I was over the intense pain I have felt over these past days, and yet, it feels as if the scab has been ripped away from my wounded heart. Everything I do is infused with the pain of our loss. I have missed Zach so much this past week!

For the weeks preceding this last one, I had been able to keep my emotions at bay, to focus on the tasks before me. That has been impossible this past week though. It seems that in everything I do, memories of Zach flood my mind:

* I'm reviewing the yearbook proofs when I come across the page with Zach's photos. I have to stop as tears blur my vision.

* I drive into North Macon Park and suddenly it hits me that this will be the first time I will coach that Zach isn't a part of it in some way.

* I watch a basketball game from the lobby. I can't make myself go in. As the girls win, I can't celebrate. Zach isn't here to share it with.

* Kemper has made the C Team baseball team. I am so proud of him! The excitement is dampened though because Zach can't tell Kemp how proud he is. Nothing seems right without Zach around to share it with. There is emptiness in my heart that will never be filled.

There were so many times during the past 18 years that we thought life was hard. We never knew how hard it could be.

I went to the cemetery with my brother Jim today. I wanted him to see the grass that Larry (Zach's grandfather) planted on Zach's grave. The grass is dormant and brown everywhere in the cemetery, except Zach's grave. You drive into the section and suddenly see this bright, vibrant patch of green rye grass amidst a field of brown. I smile whenever I see it. That grass is so alive in this place of death. It is appropriate that it covers Zach's grave.

As we were approaching the site, I couldn't see the grass.

I did not understand why until I realized that the headstone had been set. I pulled up to the curb and turned to see the stone. My heart clenched as I read the name of my firstborn. There is something about seeing it set in stone. We got out of the car and walked over to Zach's grave. Neither of us could speak as the emotion of the moment overcame us. I reminded myself that Zach was not there. He is with his Abba and as much as he loved us, he would not want to leave where he is now. After awhile we headed back to the car. I took one more look at the newly installed marker. "War Eagle" it says at the top. Zach would love it!

War Eagle Zach! I Love You!

Dad

Wednesday, February 25, 2004 11:17 AM CST

This morning I went to see the headstone for the first time. It was cold and raining. It was just like it was 11 weeks ago when we buried Zach. There was something very powerful about seeing Zach's name (my baby) on the headstone. The headstone says:

WAR EAGLE

Zachary King Morton

Z-Man

September 18, 1985

December 5, 2003

"I have fought the good fight, I have

finished the race, I have kept the faith."

II Timothy 4:7

Yes, Zach did, indeed, fight the good fight, finish the race and keep the faith.

As I stood in the rain crying I kept hearing a song by Stephen C. Chapman. It says, "We don't cry without hope, we don't say goodbye without hope. We know that goodbye is not the end. We ache with hope, grieve with hope, and let go with hope."

Yes I do ache and grieve but truly not without hope.

Clinging to Hope,

Carla

Thursday, February 26, 2004 5:43 PM CST

Today, was kind of yucky! Bless Johnny's heart he is so heavy that the pain shows on his face. We had a tough time last night as a family. We are now a broken family, and everyone is hurting in a different way. We were trying to talk about it and crying. It's like someone needs to be strong, but no one is.

I was at a hospital meeting today where a case presentation was given. The child (teenager) should not have survived the incident, but he miraculously did. He lived when by all accounts he should not have. They told about his family, and how they prayed. The focus was on all of the involved medical care. (But I focused on the prayer part.)

I thought, God we prayed. Zach wasn't "supposed" to die, but he did. Why do some get there miracle here and others do not? I really wanted to scream, why didn't we get the miracle? Questions I know, that can never be answered. Well, not on this side of eternity.

It seems that life is a challenge each and every day. I thought at first that it was awkward that people looked at me "sad" like. Like they didn't know what to say but they knew what had happened. I find that as people stop asking about us or mentioning Zach that I feel wounded. Now, I get angry wondering if someone even knows; let alone cares. I know life goes on. People around me live in their world not mine. It is painful though. It is like every encounter takes something from me. I am left empty.

Jesus, help me hang on,
Carla

Saturday, February 28, 2004 9:16 PM CST

I don't know where to begin. My heart is reeling with so many emotions. I am tired, both physically and emotionally. I am happy that FPD won the state basketball championship tonight, but I feel so empty that we could not share the moment with Zach. He so wanted to be part of a state championship team. Now I try to remind myself that he is experiencing a joy far beyond basketball. As much as my head knows that is true, my heart is heavy and empty.

Tonight was such a bittersweet experience for Carla and me. As the first half was being played, FPD was down and we were kind of glad Zach was not here. He would have been a basket case. FPD came back in the second half and as the final seconds ticked away, I could not bear to look at the FPD bench. Zach would have been so pumped! In the final moments, the FPD student section began chanting "Z-Man. Z-Man" The tears began to flow; both Carla and I were honored and touched. During the celebration time down on the court, Carla and I stood in the stands, tears streaming down our cheeks. Once again, the "Z-Man" chant started up. The tears came harder. I so envied the parents who were able to celebrate with their sons. I wanted to go down on the floor and share the moment with so many of the students I have grown to love, but my heart wouldn't let my feet move. I so hope Zach was able to see what was going on!

I am going to be taking off for a few days by myself. I need a little time to renew myself from what has been a hard two weeks. My goals are to put down everything else I have going on for a little while and let God restore me emotionally. I am so flat and empty right now. I have lost my passion for everything. I feel very ineffective as a husband, father, or teacher right now. We knew losing Zach would be painful. We never realized how emotionally empty and flat we would feel. I think the emptiness is worse than the pain because it is always there and affects everything else. Reaching for my Abba,

Johnny

Children's Grief—Are You Crying Again?

Cole asked the other night if God had raised Zach from the dead. Before I could respond, he said, "No, it's been more than 3 days. Well, maybe he's just somewhere else and we just haven't seen him yet."

Grief is strange in that you have private grief and family grief. Johnny grieves as a dad and I grieve as a mom. We grieve as his parents together. We also grieve watching the other children try to work through their own grief. These past several days have been very focused on Cole for me. He seems to be having a harder time this week. He told me the other day, {I would not stop after school and get him a drink, and we had water in the car} that he was going to die of thirst. I said, "I don't think so, if you are that thirsty then drink this water." He said, "No, I need something else." I said no again. Cole then said, "Well, you're going to lose another son because I'm going to die and then what will you think about that?" Well, how about that for a little manipulation?

Cole asked the other night if God had raised Zach from the dead. Before I could respond, he said, "No, it's been more than 3 days. Well, maybe he's just somewhere else and we just haven't seen him yet." His mind is constantly going. He cried the other night over something he could not do. He must have cried for 1 1/2 hours, really sobbing. I knew it probably was not about what he couldn't do, but about all of the strange and sad emotions he must have and not know what to do with. It's hard to watch them grieve but I know they must grieve also. Grief truly is a "work." I am beginning to understand the phrase, "grief work." It's certainly the hardest work I have ever done.

Cole had a better week this week because at his school it

was Spirit Week and they had different themes for each day. One day he got to wear his pajamas (which he slept in the night before) and didn't have to brush his hair. That really cut down on what we had to do in the morning and made it easier. One day was tacky day so he wore exactly what he wanted to and didn't brush his hair that day either. Every little thing is a blessing when it helps us "do" mornings better.

On the other hand, Kemper had tough days this week. One night he said," You know how Zach would get mad at something else sometimes and take it out at home." I said, "You mean take it out on you some time." He said, "Yes." Then he said, "That's how it's been today. I'm just taking it out on you all at home." He went on to say that he felt bad about the times he had been "mean" to Zach. We talked about that. I knew his feelings and some guilt would surface about "things" he wished he had done or not done. It gave us a little window to talk about it.

Monday, March 1, 2004 7:54 AM CST
Sunday brought bittersweet tears. The paper had a big picture of the FPD basketball players after their win. You could clearly see the black "Z" patch they wore on the jersey. There was also a picture in memory of Zach that the SSK Coldwell Banker had on their real estate page. It said, In Loving Memory, Zach Morton, Larry Kemper's grandson.

Cole asked me yesterday if Zach knew that the basketball team won. I said, "Yes I think he knows." Then Cole said, "Are you crying?" I said, "No." He said, "Are you going to cry?" He thinks every time he says Zach's name that I will cry. I can see that it is really hard for him to process things.

If you think about it, please pray for us Friday as we go to Atlanta for Cole's cardiac test. I am certain it will be a hard day for all of us. Thanks for your support. I cannot imagine how lonely the journey would be without others.

Moment by Moment, Carla

Monday, February 9, 2004 8:18 AM CST
Johnny is home sick again. It seems that we keep catching every bug. I guess our resistance is really low. Also, Cole

is having "stomach aches." He says he can't go to school because his stomach might start hurting "really" bad. I think he is just feeling very insecure. He wanted to sit on my lap this morning while I tried to put on my make-up. He was anxious all the way to school. I had to bribe him to get him to try and go for a little while. I am certain that he in no way connects these feelings with Zach being gone. His little mind and heart just know that we all went away to California and Zach did not come back. Our family is changed. That must feel scary in his little mind.

I read this statement that says, "Whatever our faith says God is, He will be." I don't think that's right. Even if my faith cannot fathom or grasp it, God is who He is. He will be who He will be. It is not dependent on me. I think that's good. I know God is so much bigger than my little mind can imagine. That's a comfort. I want to belong to a very Big God.

Hanging in there moment by moment, Carla

Cole did better this morning. He did not have a stomach ache. He was fine on the way to school. I am grateful for each little step we take. They are going to have extra recess in the afternoon. I am very thankful to Mrs. Foxworth (the principal). This should help.

Moment by Moment, Carla

Thursday, February 12, 2004 8:18 AM CST

Last night, I was praying with Kemper & Cole. We were praying for a friend of Kemper's who is sick. After we finished Cole wanted to know if he had the same thing as Kemper's friend. I said, "No you do not." He then wanted to know if that was what Zach had. I went on to tell him no and tried to explain what Zach had. He then asked, "Well what do I have?" I tried to explain what he had. He said, "Will I die from it?" Of course I said no.

Cole was also born with a congenital heart defect. His is different than Zach's but he will require open-heart surgery.

I know by his conversation that he is keenly aware of those who are "sick" that we pray for. He obviously wants to know "who will die."

We have not been to the cardiologist since Zach died. Cole will need to have a treadmill stress test that day. I know it will be hard for all of us. I don't want Cole to be scared about "his heart." It is going to be hard as we draw near the time for Cole to have surgery.

We always knew it might be hard for Cole to have to follow Zach, seeing things he went through. We of course did not imagine this outcome and Cole's potential fears. Carla

Wednesday, March 3, 2004 9:11 AM CST

Yesterday the baseball coach at FPD asked to talk with me. He said that Zach was planning on helping with baseball and was real excited about it. The coach wanted to have the team put a "Z" on the back of their helmets. He just wanted to make certain it was okay with Johnny and me. Once again, I am moved and honored that others want to remember and honor Zach. It is such a blessing.

Each day brings such a mixture of emotions. I started to cry when the coach shared that with me. Of course Cole was right with me saying, "Are you going to cry?" Are you crying?" I had just finished talking with Ria, Zach's grandmother. She had been to the gravesite. She said, "It just seems so final, when you see the headstone." She is right; it does.

So every moment, every day is a mixture of emotions, from A to Z. I guess that's why it's so draining. Carla

Wednesday, March 3, 2004 10:56 PM CST

My time away was a much needed blessing for me. It gave me time to rest my body and my mind. When I am teaching, I find that I push the grief away in order to get through the day. I steel myself against the pain so that I can get done those things that need to be done. While I was away, I had time to think about Zach and grieve. I slept, I read, and I wrote about Zach. I began putting on paper our last trip together, the train trip to California and the week before his surgery. It hurts so to remember those last days, but that time together was a gift from God and I do not want to forget any of the memories.

I returned to school with more energy today. I realize

though how draining it is to be teaching at the school right now. There are so many memories of Zach at the school. I am emotionally and physically exhausted by the time I get home. I have pictures of Zach everywhere: on my computer at home and school, sitting on my desk at school, his senior portrait in the den, and so many other places. Whenever I first see any of the photos, my initial thought is the same: How can you be gone Zach?! I am not sure I will ever get used to his absence.

I was trying to recall what Zach was doing when we had gone to a certain place. I realized that he had not been with us. The trip had been after his death. I hate creating memories that Zach is not a part of. It makes him seem so very far away. It makes me want to stop everything, and yet I know that is impossible. Death stinks for those of us left behind. Ready for Jesus to come back!

Johnny

Thursday, March 4, 2004 3:20 PM CST

Last night, I could not stop thinking about how Zach lived from 15 1/2 to 18 years of age, with the knowledge that he could die at any time. He never told anyone to our knowledge. What an unbelievable burden to bear all alone. I cannot imagine doing that when I was 15 years old. That had to be a part of why Zach had such depth.

I was thinking how amazingly balanced he stayed. Even though he apparently knew he might die, he never lived like it. I mean, he did well in school (I might not have). He applied to go to Auburn University. He took his real estate class this past summer and took the state board test after he turned 18. (He was the youngest person to have passed the real estate exam in Georgia) He always saved his money and was very frugal about what he spent. He could have lived recklessly or overly cautious. He did neither. He lived life to the max. I may be Zach's mom but I've decided that Zach is my hero. He was a bigger and wiser person than I have ever thought of being.

Missing Zach so much, Carla

When I held Zach for the first time as an infant, I would have never guessed that he would be my hero as well. What a challenge his life is to others. Thanks for sharing that story, Carla. God has used Zach to encourage and challenge me in an amazing way. I can promise you that I will never forget Zach. I share so much of his story with others!

Love,

—*Mel*

Wednesday, May 19, 2004 10:05 AM CDT

Last night Kemper was saying something about how much he loved being "on line" on the computer talking to friends. I said, "Yes, I know that's why we take it away when you are disobedient." He smiled and said, "No, really I don't like it that much." I said, "You don't fool me. That's why we would take Zach's phone (or threaten it) if we ever needed to." Kemper said, "Zach would just die if he lost his phone." Then Kemper said, "I would probably have faked it and said Oh, my heart hurts. I feel bad." Before I could respond Kemper said, "But Zach never did that. He was too nice for that." We talked about how Zach never used his condition for any excuse. He never wanted attention drawn to it. He so wanted to fit in and be normal. I told Kemper about that time when he was in 4th or 5th grade and some of the boys made fun of him at P.E. and said that he just used his heart problem so he would not have to do P.E. Kemper said, "Like he wouldn't have given anything to play at P.E." Yes, he would have! As you can tell my heart is heavy with missing Zach. Thanks for letting me share my memories and my pain.

So wanting to talk to my baby, Carla

J&C—Thank you, again, for sharing your hurting hearts. As I sit here with tears flowing, I continue to pray for God to bind up those broken hearts and give you beauty for ashes. What a TRUE BLESSING to have an 18 year old son be your hero. Zach's love for life was a blessing to everyone he was around. My heart so aches for that missing piece in your family.

—*Betsy*

71

Friday, March 5, 2004 8:02 PM CST

We received a good report from Cole's visit to the cardiologist today. Cole did great on the stress test and the doctor cleared him to play baseball. We know that someday Cole will face surgery, but we give thanks it is not now. I don't think we could handle another surgery right now.

We knew that Cole was not looking forward to going to the doctor. In his mind, Zach went to the doctor and did not come back home. He has already asked if he was going to die like Zach did. Carla said that Cole's attitude was much improved after the good report. I wish I could know what is going on in that mind of his. We are left to trust that God will be whatever Cole needs Him to be right now.

Johnny

P.S. It's about 2:00 AM now and, not too surprising, I am still up. Weekend nights are so hard for me. I spent so many nights waiting up for Zach that even now I don't want to go to bed until I know he's home. It makes for long nights. Like the last moments of a vacation or saying goodbye to a loved one, I want to hold onto Zach as long as possible. When I finally crawl into bed in the early hours of the morning, it always hits me like a ton of bricks...Zach won't ever come home late again. I won't hear his car driving up. I won't hear his key in the door. I won't hear him say "I'm home." How I hate these nights. It hurts so much!

Pray for the Boys

*"I know what I'm going to ask for next Christmas.
I'm going to ask for Zach back."*

—Cole

Tuesday, April 13, 2004 4:04 PM CDT

God is unchangeable, therefore He is just as loving when I cannot feel Him or see Him. I must cling to that and dare not trust my emotions at this time. Cole said on the way to school today that he missed Zach. Then all of a sudden he said, "I know what I'm going to ask for next Christmas. I'm going to ask for Zach back." Oh, if only it could be so. (I realize that this does maybe present a picture that Cole thinks Santa is very powerful) I guess I will need to work on this.

Hanging On, Carla

Carla, One of the many things you told me when I was in the hospital with a child with a serious diagnosis was to grieve as long as I needed to and that it was ok to do that. Your words were so comforting to me.

—Katherine

Monday, March 15, 2004 8:15 AM CST

Cole went with me to Zach's grave yesterday for the first time. He asked as we drove in if I was going to cry. (That's his standard question) I told him I would try not to. When we got there he said, "Why didn't we get Zach one of those BIG monuments?" I said well, we got him a nice one with an eagle on it. Cole said, "I think one of those big ones would have been better." Cole did think that Zach's green grass was really cool. I told him that "Big" had planted it. He said, "Way to go

'Big' (that's my dad)." Cole wanted to water all of the grass so we did. It was bittersweet.

Hanging On,
Carla

Monday, April 12, 2004 1:09 PM CDT
Cole is still very clingy and did not want to go to school today. Anything that is a change of any sort throws Cole off. Yesterday, for some reason he asked more questions about Zach than he has thus far. He asked why he and Zach had to have a heart problem. I reassured him that his was not as bad, as Zach's. Cole said, "I wish Zach could have had what I have." He asked why we had to go to California and why we could not have stayed here. He talked about them trying to "fix" Zach but that his blood pressure went down and he had to go back to the (Emergency Room) and that was why he died. It was good that he talked freely for a few minutes about Zach and what happened. I realized obviously, that he (at age 7) does not really understand what happened. Also, I will have to be careful about saying the Emergency Room since that's where he thinks Zach went and died. I tried to explain some things but lost him by that point. It is just below the surface with both boys. Pray we will be sensitive to each time and opportunity to "work" through the grief as they are ready and need to. Carla

Thursday, May 27, 2004 6:35 AM CDT
Cole wanted to move into Zach's room. He said, that he thought Zach would not mind since he wasn't here and also that Cole liked Auburn. I told him we would just make room for some of his stuff in Zach's room for now. He seems excited to have Zach's room. Maybe in some way this is helpful for him. On the whole Cole has seemed a little more like himself but still is clingy at times. The other night Johnny and I had walked out to sit on the porch. We told Cole but apparently he did not hear us. A few minutes later I hear this screaming. Cole was upset and crying because he could not find us. (Kemper was in the bathroom, but apparently did not feel the need to respond to Cole) He does not like me to leave him

74

really. He definitely does not feel a comfort level with Kemper watching him....go figure.

We are just inching along; weary, a lot of days with this work of grief. I think it must be like having to eat a big elephant; one yucky bite at a time.

Hanging On, Carla

Sunday, May 30, 2004 3:52 PM CDT

I know that some of the reactions of the boys are because we are all in grief and adjusting. But, right now my patience seems so thin. I am weary. Kemper is 13. (That probably says enough). These are probably difficult days for him, but it is definitely a challenge for me. Cole's response to most of life is to ask why, or why not; about everything.

Even when I do provide an answer it is not enough. Right now they are both sort of beating me down. Please pray that I will be given what I need for each moment. I don't want to fail with these two, but I really want to crawl up in bed with my grief and be selfish. Carla

Tuesday, June 15, 2004 7:03 AM CDT

Cole really seems to be having a hard time these last few weeks. He may be sensing my grief. He has been very clingy, and very insecure. He wants to stay just right under me. He kisses and kisses me at night. He asks for me to stay home everyday I have to go to work. He is afraid that I will leave him. He stays on the verge of tears.

He cannot really express what is going on. He probably doesn't even know.

It is so difficult to grieve (which is really very self focused) and meet the children's needs. We are trying to be balanced but it is hard.

This morning I heard a song I have mentioned before. It says "the road is long and the climb is steep, come and give me hope Lord." Right now that is what I need—hope. The road looks so long and so bleak.

Hanging by a thread, Carla

Thursday, June 24, 2004 7:52 AM CDT

I do "feel" as if some of the heaviness has lifted for the moment. I will not question it but just try to appreciate it while it lasts. It is such a bummer to be heavy all the time. For the lighter moments I am grateful.

Please continue to pray for the boys. Cole still seems to be having a hard time. His response is to be very clingy and very "uncertain" of everything. He is most unhappy when I have to leave to go to work. (But, we must eat). I believe that he is grieving but it so hard to know exactly what to do. It is hard to see the children hurt and not be able to "fix" it. I know they must grieve and "feel" the pain & loss as we have to. Carla

Friday, July 2, 2004 7:00 AM CDT

This week has been a very stark reminder of Zach's absence. It was Cole's 8th birthday on Wednesday. Zach would have made a big deal about it for him. He would have taken him to do something he wanted to do that day. We actually had his party earlier and so Wednesday was sort of a day that was hard to make special. I felt like it was just flat. I just couldn't seem to make it happen. Kemper has also been out of town so it's been very strange. It's like I wish I had done better, made the day more special or something. (You struggle with guilt about how you're doing with the other children). Carla

Monday, July 12, 2004 2:33 PM CDT

I feel like my few days of not feeling as bad have gone. I find that I am back feeling exhausted all of the time. I will have slept well all night (a lot of hours) and I wake up and still feel tired. I hate feeling tried all of the time. I know it is part of the process but I hate it. As always it seems that there is a constant mixture of emotions.

I worry about Cole and how this will have affected him when all is said and done. I know that I am not being consistent with him like I should. I know this in my mind, but it is so hard to follow through when you feel so drained. I feel pressure (pressure that I probably am putting on myself) to

76

not mess up with the children. I find myself struggling every-day to do with them the things I should. I need for Cole to read to me everyday (well that's what the teacher said). I need to get him to obey me the first time, not the tenth. I need to read the Bible & pray with him at night. I need to help him not "whine" all of the time. The list on paper doesn't look too bad but somehow most days I am too overwhelmed to make it happen. Carla

Sunday, August 1, 2004 8:12 PM CDT
Cole seems to really have been doing a lot of "grief" work. He was in bed with me the other night when he started say-ing that he was too scared to go to sleep. As we talked it came out that he is afraid that he will go to sleep and die. He said that we said that Zach was asleep and then he died. Cole said, "How do you know I will not go to sleep and die?" I would try and reassure him and he would say "But what if I do die?" He had all kinds of questions about heaven and how would he find Zach and who would meet him there. He asked about his own heart problem and how did I know he would not die also. He asked if you had Jesus in your heart but you did something bad (like if you stole something) would you still go to heaven? He asked about babies and little kids if they went to heaven. He asked about animals and where they went. He wanted to know when I thought I would go to heav-en and everyone else in the family. He kept saying, "But I'm scared I'm going to die." What does it feel like to die? How do you just die? Did Zach know he was going to die? Was Zach scared? If Zach didn't know he was going to die then why did he tell you to tell Kemper & me that he loved us? Didn't you pray for Zach to be healed?"
Wow..............This went on for one and a half hours. I could not believe the depth of questions, the concern, the fear, the pain over Zach being gone. He kissed and kissed on me and kept hugging. I did not want to cry because I want-ed him to talk and get it out. (I was praying so for wisdom.) He would ask (we were lying in the dark) are you crying? I would say no and then he would get still for a few minutes and then start again. He told me to wake him up the next

morning to make certain that he didn't die...........

I am grateful that some of his anxious thoughts came to the surface. But it was hard to see how this has so affected him. I just pray that God will bore deep into his soul during this time. As you think about it pray for Cole and his ability to grieve as he needs to but also feel some sense of security.

Each day is a journey. Thanks for traveling with us. Carla

Wednesday, September 8, 2004 11:41 AM CDT

Cole got a toothache and started running fever. Of course it's a holiday and then the power is out across town due to the "hurricane effects." We ended up having to go to another dentist that could get us in, finding out the tooth had abscessed and then having to go to an oral surgeon to have it extracted yesterday. Cole will definitely not win patient of the year. He is more melodramatic than you can imagine. He continues to cry and talk about dying, going to heaven, wish he wasn't born etc. It is definitely draining. Before they put him to "sleep" (laughing gas) yesterday, he was lying there on the table and kept saying he loved me. Just like Zach had done. It was way too close to home. That whole thing about undid me. I am weary from grief and life right now.

Weary and really too tired to hang on, (grateful that He holds me),

Carla

78

Weeping in the Night

We both came to the decision that if God is not God during our deepest pain and sorrow, then He is not God at all.

—Johnny

Sunday, March 7, 2004 5:50 PM CST

I am still amazed at how unfocused I am. For someone who normally is focused and on task this is so strange. I have realized that a lot of my questions lately have been not why, but what is this all for? What is the purpose behind everything we have and are living through? So much of my purpose in the last 18 years has been caring for Zach. I was constantly aware and assessing "how" he was doing. It's like someone said to me, "Carla, I cannot begin to imagine the loss that you feel as someone who has literally breathed every breath for their precious child." She was so on target, and I really didn't even realize it until Zach was gone. Much of my focus and purpose was caring for Zach.

Of course I know and certainly love and care for my other two boys. But so much of what I did and who I became, was wrapped up in Zach. It's hard to explain, but I feel so "at odds." God will have to direct me in time. For now I must just live in this wilderness.

On a lighter note to demonstrate just how "unfocused" I am, I will tell my latest tale. We were at a restaurant, and I went to the ladies bathroom. Only, it was the men's. I opened the door, and there stood a man (just his back, was all I could see) but I just stood there with the door open. It was like, (one-one thousand, two-one thousand, three-one thousand, (my thought) that is a man, four-one-thousand, (next thought) this must be a man's bathroom, five-one thousand,

79

(last thought) I should close the door.) I did and finally found where I should be. But of course you can see how SLOW..............things are moving through my fog. When I got back to the table, I told my mom. She said, "Are you certain you should be out?" No, I'm not certain at all that I should be out......... Hanging on, Carla

Monday, March 8, 2004 7:42 PM CST
We took the high school students to see "The Passion" movie today. In addition to the scourging of Christ, two scenes hit me the hardest. The first was as Jesus was falling during His trek to Golgotha and we saw Mary flashback to when Jesus was a little boy. The emotional bond between parents who hurt as they watch their child suffer reminded me so much of Zach. For 18 years we hurt with him knowing there was little we could do to stop his pain. I know a little of the helplessness I am sure Mary felt as she watched Jesus bear our sins. I thought the movie did a great job of portraying the special relationship between a parent and child.

The second scene that deeply affected me was as the nails were being driven into the flesh of Jesus and He utters those incredible words of forgiveness, "Father forgive them. They don't understand what they are doing." They didn't, but I do. How many times do I choose to do something that I know goes against God's desire for me? I knowingly sin even as I understand that it was my sin that put Jesus on the cross. The incredible thing is that Christ died for me knowing the somewhat cavalier attitude I would have in regard to sin AFTER He had saved me. What an awesome God we serve and how truly amazing His grace is.

Johnny

Wednesday, March 10, 2004 8:27 AM CST
I have had such a mix of emotions and thoughts the last two days. I read something on grief that really is on target. It said that when you are grieving it is like having a note stuck on the front of your brain. Every single thought has to filter through the note. The note says something like, "Zach is

gone. I can't believe Zach is dead. My child has died." Everything you do and think all day is filtered through that note. I think it is such a good description of how the mind works during this time.

Last night I kept waking up and seeing Zach the way he was right before he died. The way he looked. His eyes were so big they looked like saucers. He was trying to talk around the ventilator. The look on his face, I can't describe it. But, for some reason I kept seeing it all night long. I woke up tired from the night. For some reason my mind must need to "work" through some of these images.

Holding On, Carla

Saturday, March 13, 2004 10:00 AM CST

I feel like I am coming unglued. It's is so strange. This grief work, it's like on one hand it's the sadness, sorrow over missing Zach. But, on the other hand even when you are focused on something else it's this all "draining" experience. Just living is taking all I have. Even something that seems like it would be fun, ends up being hard. It is just plain exhausting. It seems unfair to have to have this "life sucking" force at the same time you're sad. I know its part of the same thing, but it really feels like two different things are going on. I hate it.

I realized yesterday and today that my last nerve has been stepped on and is gone. Yesterday, I tried to go to the DQ and order a quart of ice cream and some hot fudge sauce. (To bring home, not just for me....) They would not sell me the sauce. They have before and I tried to explain that. They even brought the manager to the window to explain to me that they never sell toppings by themselves. Well, it made me so mad. I started to cry. As much as I love hot fudge, I know I'm over the edge when I cry about it. Later, when I told someone, she said, "Were you at the DQ?" I said, "Yes." She said," I thought you were going to say you looked up and were at Hardee's or something." My reputation is totally shot. My prayer today is just for Jesus to hold on to me. I can't even hold on to Him. Carla

Friday, March 19, 2004 7:39 AM CST

"Therefore, since we are surrounded by so great a cloud of witnesses ... let us run with endurance the race that is set before us." Hebrews 12:1

Because Zach couldn't participate in sports, Kemper and Cole were his extension. He was their biggest cheerleader. When they had success, Zach celebrated with them and bragged to anyone who would listen. When they did not, he felt their pain. Kemper ran in his first track meet yesterday. He ran the 1600m race and came in second by a stride, finishing with the same time as the winner. I was so proud and my first thought was "I wish Zach was here." The Hebrews verse came to mind and I realized, in a way, Zach is here. A part of him will always be with Carla, Kemper, Cole and me. I think he was cheering Kemper on to the finish line. Kemper said it was the encouragement of the crowd that pushed him on to the finish. I'd like to think Zach was part of that. It was an encouragement to know that Zach was part of that cloud of witnesses.

We had our NCAA basketball tournament draft. For the past several years, Zach, and I had joined King and five other guys in making picks for the tournament. Zach loved it. "March Madness" was one of his favorite times of the year. This year, Kemper took Zach's place. I was dreading the evening without Zach there. I was relieved when it was not as bad as I had feared. We talked about Zach and laughed about things that had happened in the past. One guy, Marsh, told about how one year Zach was in first after the first round, but had lost all his teams by the end of the second round. When Zach's last team lost, Marsh called up Zach and ragged him about being out. (Zach would have done the same.) When Marsh got off the phone, his wife reprimanded him, "Do you realize you were just harassing a 15 year old?" It was Ok though. Zach had a unique ability to be peers with adults. Zach loved it that Marsh would call him up and treat him just like anyone else in the group. I don't know that I ever thanked Marsh for doing that.

Remembering the joy, Johnny

82

Saturday, March 20, 2004 5:10 PM CST

Zach would have loved today. I realize his day in heaven is better than any day here, but he would have loved Macon today. It's pretty here today. A beautiful spring day, Zach would have been in hog heaven. He would have the top down on his car. I drove it today. I wished so that he could be driving and me riding with him. I was thinking about him and thinking how brown his face would already be. He always tanned very easily. I really wanted to think about "what if." What if he had survived the surgery and he was better. What fun we would have enjoyed with him having the physical strength to experience new things. Oh, how I wish that had been the plan. How I wish he could be here. I can't stay there very long in my mind. It's too painful. I wanted to get to have him experience some healing on this side. I wanted to get to see the joy and pleasure he would have been. Oh how I yearn to see him and talk to him.

Hanging On, Carla

Monday, March 22, 2004 2:47 PM CST

Man, today has been so overwhelming for some reason. I just feel like a truck hit me. I realize that the smallest things can just overwhelm me. Tasks that I would have tackled with a vengeance before are just too big to handle. Life just seems too much. The house, the yard, laundry, and even feeding the cat are such "jobs." There is no energy to "go after things." I am constantly amazed at how draining this grief work is.

I dreamed about Zach last night. It was not a good dream. I kept seeing him "looking" bad. He was so thin, and his nails looked so blue. He was out of breath. I know it's not true but it is disturbing to wake up and realize what I have dreamed.

Cole's teacher told me that he has seemed "distant" the last few weeks. She feels like he is grieving. It's hard to try and balance everything and watch diligently over Cole and Kemper. What I really wish I could do is crawl in bed for a couple of weeks. It's so hard, just to get by.

Needing to be Carried, Carla

Tuesday, March 23, 2004 10:08 PM CST

I have the privilege of leading a spiritual renewal emphasis at FPD. These past two days in chapel, I have had the chance to share with our students some of what God has taught me these past years, much of it through Zach. I shared the truth that everything in life is about God's glory, not us. Even the cross, being the means of our salvation, is about Jesus being glorified for His sacrifice. Jesus is the focus, not us. I talked about how it is easy to give God honor and glory when things are good in our lives.

Tomorrow, I will be discussing that even in the midst of our deepest trials and sorrows, it's not about us....It is still about God's glory. The question is whether I am willing to give God what His due is when my heart is broken. That is the question Carla and I both faced in the hours after Zach's death. We both came to the decision that if God is not God during our deepest pain and sorrow, then He is not God at all. We committed ourselves to seeing God glorified in the midst of our pain.

I want the students to know that it is in giving God glory during times such as this that we are lifted with God. Even as I relived those awful early morning hours after Zach's death, I see God's hand of love. Believing, Johnny

Friday, March 26, 2004 10:21 PM CST

This past week, I have been taken back to the days surrounding Zach's death. I have relived those moments in my head and as I read the emails people sent us. These are some moments that are forever frozen in my mind:

* Seeing him and Carla sobbing on the edge of the bed after his heart cath.

* Hearing him tell us that he had known for two years that he might die.

* Standing at the rail together at Pier 39 in San Francisco, we listened to a saxophone play Christmas carols the night before his surgery.

* Watching Zach tell Carla & me he loved us via sign language after the first surgery.

This week, I realized that I was getting used to Zach's

absence. I hate that! It means he has been gone a long time, almost four months. I miss him terribly, like a thirst that cannot be quenched. But I am oh so grateful for the memories that fill my head and heart. All of them, either of joy or pain, keep Zach with me.

Sitting in the lap of my Abba,

Johnny

Sunday, March 28, 2004 10:29 PM CST

"Christ in you, the hope of glory." Colossians 1:26

Whatever we do, wherever we go, the thought that we miss Zach is at the forefront of our minds. It remains the filter through which everything else must pass. Zach is gone.

I shared with a friend the other day that the one of the things we must cling to is hope. We have hope that we will be with Zach one day. We have hope that the pain will ease while the sweetness of the memories remain. We have hope that we will not have to go through this again. We have hope that others will never forget our sweet Zach. We have hope that Kemper and Cole will know God as intimately as Zach did. We have hope that God has a plan for us to use what He has taught us and built into us during these long months to bring glory to Himself. We have hope that our sorrows will not be wasted. And in all of our hopes, we know that Jesus himself is the guarantor of our hope

Clinging to hope, Johnny

Tuesday, March 30, 2004 8:57 AM CST

As I write this entry, King and Katie (Carla's brother and sister-in-law) are in the hospital awaiting the arrival of their second child. Carla is there helping with the delivery. I am reminded in all of this that life goes on. New life is always exciting. The joy of the new baby will lighten the heaviness we all feel, if only for awhile. Zach would have been the most excited of all of us, other than King and Katie. He so loved King. I am sorry that this new addition will never know his cousin Zach in this life. Celebrating life, new and past! Johnny

Trusting in the Dark

*One of the things I really struggle with is the absolute
silence of God during this time. It's apparent to me....
God just gets to be God. I don't get to understand.*

—Carla

Wednesday, April 7, 2004 10:04 PM CDT

This was our first spring break without Zach. His presence was so powerfully "absent." At moments I thought I would not be able to catch my breath because the ache was so heavy. I miss him so. I cannot stand the thought of not seeing him for who knows how long. I know when I get there it will seem like it has been no time at all, but now it seems like a lot. It has been 4 months since Zach died. At moments, it still seems so unreal. I just can't believe he is gone. I miss his "deep" voice and his belly laugh where he could hardly get his breath.

This grief thing is the pits. It just keeps on keeping on. This week I thought about the saying. "You can run but you can't hide." Grief is like that. I can change locations or try and do something different, but it finds you. You can't escape the pain. I'm pretty certain I would if I could.

Hanging on, Carla

It is comforting to know that Godly people have weak, "human" moments too. There is no other feeling in this world to compare to this grief. But...it does SLOWLY wane over time; ever present but not eternally as overwhelming.

—Kristi

Friday, April 9, 2004 10:53 PM CDT

This the first time I have posted in about a week. My spirit is so heavy. I have tried to write, but no words would come. Words seem inadequate to express the darkness I am feeling. We seemed to have moved into a time of perpetual heaviness. Maybe it is the rapid succession of "firsts" we are going through now; everything on the horizon seems to magnify Zach's absence.

Everywhere I have gone these past weeks, images of Zach surround me. I close my eyes and I can see him, hear his voice. I open them—nothing. I miss him so much. I feel so empty. It's like the man in the desert dying of thirst. He sees mirages and full of hope he reaches for the water, only to come up with a handful of sand. That's how I feel. It seems that I can see and hear Zach, but then nothing. The song says it best. What I would give for "One More Day" with my son.

Weeping in the night, Johnny

Saturday, April 10, 2004 10:20 PM CDT

Tomorrow is Easter. Though I do not feel like it, I will go worship in the morning and spend the afternoon with family and friends. I don't feel like celebrating Christ's resurrection, but I will. In the midst of my grief, I will worship not because I feel like it, but because it pleases God. Easter reminds me that this life is not about me and my grief, it is all about God. As I celebrate Christ's death and resurrection, I am reminded and comforted that one day there will be another resurrection. I can't wait!

Celebrating Jesus even in our pain,
Johnny & Carla

I looked at the hearts on the homepage of the web site that say, "God is love" and was so reminded of the heart of Zach which was filled with life and love from our Father because of his relationship with Jesus. I rejoice in Zach's demonstration of God's love.

—Gwen

87

Monday, April 12, 2004 1:09 PM CDT

I heard someone talk about how at times our pain and sorrow are so compelling, and so absorbing that "they" feel more real than God. I think that is right. I know it is not true, but at times the pain does "feel" more real than God. This is the strangest spiritual place I have ever been. I do not want to miss out on anything God is doing in this time in our lives, but at the same time I am totally void of much feeling or emotions. I feel flat and empty on the inside. I dare not trust my feelings at all, during this time.

Hanging On,
Carla

Your love and your openness continues to ground me in holding on tightly to what we all should do with every breath we take and every moment we spend in the "waiting room"... turning our eyes upon Jesus! I miss Zach, but continue to hold on to the blessings he brought me and the conversations we shared.

—Rhonda

Thursday, April 15, 2004 8:30 PM CDT

I have been reading a book called, "Sit Down God! I'm Angry!" It is by a father who lost his son at 17. While much of our stories are different, something I read last night resonated with me. After a loss such as we have experienced with Zach, our natural reaction is to stop living. We want to hole up and hide away. Obviously we can't do that. Life goes on, even in times of death. There are bills to pay, Kemper and Cole to raise, ball games, just everyday living. Sometimes, as I look back, I wonder if I should have stayed at First Presbyterian Day School. Maybe I could have taken a leave for the rest of the year. I knew it would be hard to keep teaching at the school where Zach attended. I did not realize how draining it would be.

I teach only juniors and seniors. As a senior, Zach was scheduled to be in my 2nd period class. I so enjoyed having him in my classes. (He liked it too! He was never embarrassed to be in my class.) It has been so hard watching the

88

other seniors go on. Today, the seniors picked up their graduation announcements.

I won't be going to senior honors night or graduation. Sometimes I close my eyes and imagine Zach walking down the aisle at graduation. I can see the huge smile he would be wearing. At times, I still can't believe he is gone. For the early parts of Zach's life, we never dreamed he would see his graduation. I remember when he was scheduling classes when he first went to FPD, I told the advisor to not worry too much about what he took. He probably would not make it. Prophetic as it now seems, 6 months ago we couldn't imagine Zach not being here for these major events. He was so alive and looking forward to graduating and going to Auburn in the fall. How fragile life is and how quickly dreams can be shattered. Johnny

Monday, April 19, 2004 9:08 AM CDT

One of the things that I really struggle with is the absolute silence of God during this time. I want to hear from Him but it is just so dark and quiet. I do think maybe one of the things that is becoming more apparent to me is that God just gets to be God. I don't get to understand. I read this morning, "We need the kind of faith whose God is so big as to be not just unmanageable, but to a large extent (this sounds paradoxical to the Christian ears) unknowable." I don't really like it, but I think it's the way it is. The same section in this book on Job said, "As we progress in faith we go through times when we are less and less certain that we really know Him at all, and yet more certain than ever that He knows us. It is easier to diminish God than to enlarge one's own heart." Mike Mason, "The Gospel According to Job."

God will have to enlarge my heart. Thanks for praying and caring. Carla

Wednesday, April 21, 2004 11:37 AM CDT

One of the reasons losing a child is so difficult is that you grieve not only the present loss, but you also grieve what would have been. The season we find ourselves in now is living through many of those future events that we had dreamed of experiencing with Zach, but which now only emphasize the magnitude of our loss. I am so envious of the other parents who get to experience these last events of high school. The pain of our loss is as acute as it has ever been.

I know we will get through these difficult days. I also know that we will always wonder what they might have been if God's plan was different. For now we cling to His promises, trusting in His grace for moment by moment strength and trusting even in the dark.

Clinging, Johnny

You prove that following God is all that is important—through the darkness and through the uncertainty.

—*Theresa*

Thursday, April 22, 2004 7:56 AM CDT

I must be moving into the anger/irritability phase. It seems like my fuse is so short and people and life keep lighting it. Yesterday was just one of those days. I found that everything made me so mad. Last week it was the toilet, now the water/sprinkler/hose would not work. I was going under the house to try and see if the water was cut off and I did not duck enough. I hit the wallboard at a nice pace. It knocked me all the way to the ground, broke the visor I had on and dazed me. I could not believe it. I thought, I am passed out in the yard behind the house and no one will know.

Later I was on the other side of town and realized I did not have any cash. I realize that most people are very savvy at ATM machines. I am not one of them. I don't like machines that talk to me and I have to remember codes. Well, anyway I could not find an ATM machine. I thought they were supposed to be everywhere. When I did, it would not take my card. It took me 4 machines before it worked. By now it has taken me an hour and I am "hot". I know it's life but it's like I have no tolerance for it at all.

Hanging by a very thin, short fuse,
Carla

Tuesday, April 27, 2004 6:11 AM CDT

I was thinking over the past days how tired this whole grieving process makes you feel. There are days when you sleep all night, but you still seem to have no energy to do anything. I realized it is probably because everyday you experience that day in terms of past, present, and future. During grief, you live three days for every one day. You experience it as it was when Zach was here. You remember all the times past. Then you live the day in the reality of the present. You experience what the loss means; picking up the boys when Zach would have done it, the empty spot at the dinner table. And then finally, you live the day in light of the future that will not be. You think of future times and then realize that Zach won't be there. You alter plans accordingly. To me that is the hardest of all. This three-in-one living takes its toll. You realize how much you need God to carry you from day to day. Thankfully, He is faithful to do just that.

Trusting in my Abba,
Johnny

Wednesday, April 28, 2004 11:11 AM CDT

Yesterday I went to get gas, I stood at the pump for several minutes trying to make it come on. Then, I saw the sign that said, "Pay inside first." (Here we go again). So I go pay. Then I go back and try to start. It still will not start. I spend several more minutes and then go back inside. I ask the lady behind the desk. She said, "Are you certain your pushing the red button?" I'm thinking "this is really bad". So I go back out and start again. Yes, I am pushing the red button. Now, I also push every other button because nothing is happening. Then, for the 3rd time I go back into the store. (She of course is on the phone each time...I don't think it had to do with gas). This time I tell her it is still not working. She says, can you just drive around to another pump? So, I go move the car and start over. I would have left but I've already paid my money. Finally after 20 minutes I am able to pump the gas.

Now, I go to Kroger, just for a few items. I give the cashier the Kroger plus card as I go through the line. The total rang up more than I thought it should be. When I saw the total I

91

said, "Did you scan my Kroger plus card?" I asked.

She said, "No."

I asked, "Well can you scan it now?"

She answered, "No, you have to go to customer service to do that."

I just said, "Never mind." I thought, "You people win." As I walked to the car, I thought, I know this is not heaven, Lord, and I know we try for it to be and it will not, but I'm thinking it may be a little closer to Hell.

Barely Hanging On, Carla

Graduation

The senior class dedicated the yearbook to Zach.

"...But more than memories is the legacy he left us. He challenged us to entrust our souls to a faithful Creator. He convicted us with his courage.... He taught us that God is too good to be unkind and too wise to be mistaken. He inspired us to value what is really important in life."

Saturday, May 1, 2004 4:04 PM CDT

This week I went to get flowers to place at the grave. As my mama and I were looking for flowers I said, "We should be out getting a graduation gift, not flowers for his grave." It was a tearful day as we tended his grave. I would so love a bear hug from Zach. For those of you who he hugged (and there were a lot of you) he gave the strongest bear-hug of anyone I've ever known. I need one. Carla

Tuesday, May 4, 2004 4:20 PM CDT

Today was a bittersweet day for all of us. The school had a special assembly to have a preview slide show of the yearbook. Unknown to us, the school had invited all of our family to be at the assembly. The senior class dedicated the yearbook to Zach. They read a beautiful tribute to him that will also appear in the yearbook. I wanted to share what they said today.

In Loving Memory
Zachary King Morton
Class of 2004

He is in the heart of each of us. We will remember his "high fives," his love of Auburn University, his unbelievable knowledge of sports statistics, his smiles and his jokes. But more than memories is the legacy he left us. He challenged us to entrust our souls to a faithful Creator. He convicted us with his courage. He lifted us with his humor.

He had an infectious smile that reached into the soul. He loved his family and friends. He embraced life. He never met a stranger and he never made an enemy. He was (and is) our inspiration. He made us thankful for every breath. He taught us that God is too good to be unkind and too wise to be mistaken. He inspired us to value what is really important in life.

From his birth he was set apart, captured by a Holy calling which drew him near to the Lord. His time here with us was far too short but his place in heaven is eternal. We are blessed to have called him our friend. We take with us into the future not only his memory but his life verse, which is hidden in our hearts. "And we know that God causes all things to work together for good to those who love God, to those who are called according to His purpose." (Romans 8:28)

We dedicate this 2004 Reflections Yearbook to our classmate and friend,

Zach Morton.
We love you Z-Man!
The Class of 2004

It was a beautiful and kind tribute to Zach. As Johnny said today, "It was a privilege to know Zach."

My soul cries & the tears flow, Carla

What a challenge to those of us left behind. What a legacy Zach left. Most people will live a long life on this earth and never hear such words of love, respect and admiration. He touched the lives of people you will never meet this side of heaven. Zach fulfilled his purpose on earth and he finished well! What a joy to meet the Creator and have no regrets!

—Melanie

Wednesday, May 5, 2004 10:41 PM CDT

As I read the guest book, I am continually amazed by the things people say. Numerous times people have commented about being encouraged by our faith and walk with God. I find that strange because I don't feel that I am doing all that well many times. I feel like people will see a man stuck in grief and self-pity instead of trusting and resting in God. I was reading a book by John Eldridge not long ago that talked about us allowing others to see the glory of God within us. I guess that is what God has been doing these past months, letting people see His glory revealed in the midst of our pain. I guess it is like Paul said, our weakness allows God to reveal His glory in us. That is ultimately what life is about—God's glory!

Trying to live, Johnny

Saturday, May 8, 2004 1:03 PM CDT

I think every holiday is hard but Mother's Day was the pits. I want to be the mother of 3 children that are all here. For some reason I cannot get this image out of my mind. When Zach was about 2 or 3, he was in the preschool class. One day I got there to pick him up and I looked through the window pane of the door. All of the children were on their mats in a circle. All of the children were standing up on their mats and singing a song with hand motions. Zach was sitting down on his mat with his little legs crossed. He was breathing heavily. He apparently was too tired to stand up and sing. He was just sitting and watching the other children. He looked so thrilled to just watch them. I felt so sad as I watched him sit on his mat while everyone else could move around. I will never forget how precious he looked (I know everyone thinks their child is precious, but I think this one was really true...he had white-blonde hair and these big eyes. He would get such a tan in the summer) Anyway, I so wanted to help him. It just broke my heart.

I realize now that much of Zach's life was like that picture that day. He sat, watched and enjoyed while others around him did things he could never do. I cannot let go of that picture. I so wish I could have made his life easier. He suffered, but he did it silently and alone. He very seldom ever let us see his suffering. I ache to reach into the picture in my mind and pick him up and take him away from all the hurt.

My mother's heart hurts today. I miss him so.

Crying, Carla

Monday, May 10, 2004 7:58 AM CDT

To help keep things in prospective, God gave me Cole. He had some precious things from school that he had made me. As I read what he wrote about me, I would say, "That is so sweet, thank you." Cole would then reply, "The teacher made us say that!" One of the things they answered was "What is the funniest thing that has happened to your mother." Cole wrote, "When her hair turned 'black.'" (I don't know who has been talking with this child) but anyway, he keeps me humble.

Glad it's Monday (believe it or not)

Carla

Tuesday, May 11, 2004 9:44 AM CDT

Today and yesterday have been incredibly hard days. I was OK until yesterday morning when they called for seniors to go get their caps and gowns. Zach would have come back to show me his. I would have given him grief about having to wear red for his graduation. Later in the day they rang the last bell for the seniors. The seniors then gathered for pictures and goodbyes. I was supposed to take pictures, but I could not bear to be there.

For the longest time, we never imagined Zach would get to graduation. We finally started to believe he might make it. We thought we would see him finish. We never knew that the course God had set for him would be finished. To be so close makes this time all the more difficult though. I have spent so much time these past days imagining what if... I wish I could stop because the pain is so intense.

Thanks for listening! Thanks for caring!

Clinging to my Abba! Johnny

Friday, May 14, 2004 9:09 PM CDT

We continue to experience and learn new aspects of this grieving process. During the early months, I found that the pain of missing Zach was a welcome thing. It gave me an emotional connection with Zach. I have come to the point where I long to be able to remember Zach without the pain. I want to enjoy the memories, but not hurt so much. I am also seeing how self-centered grief is. I am hurting. I miss Zach. I want to be with him. During the grief process, I look at most things in how they relate to ME. I don't want Zach back for his sake; I want him for mine.

Trusting, Johnny

Monday, May 17, 2004 5:59 PM CDT

As I left the store after seeing a graduating senior and her mother, I thought to myself, "I hope that mom realizes how blessed she is today. She is getting ready to see her daughter graduate. How I wish that was me." I hope seeing me reminded her of what she has. I hope she will tell her kids she loves them and hold them a little closer. Death changes your perspective. It makes you realize what is truly important and how quickly it can be taken away. I never wanted to be known as the father of the boy who died, but maybe God will use that for good, if it reminds folks to cherish what they have.

My heart is heavy, Johnny

Friday, May 21, 2004 6:06 AM CDT

Dear Zach,

Tomorrow would be your graduation day. I can imagine what the day would be like. Crazy comes to mind. I can hear your mom warning me I better not be late as I tried to convince her I could coach Cole's playoff game at 1:00 and still get to graduation. You'd have been on my side. In fact, you would be mad that you could not go to the game. You always were Kemper and Cole's biggest cheerleader.

At graduation, I would have been rushing to get my cap and gown on. I would have ragged you to no end about wearing red to graduate. I can hear you laughing about it now.

(You always did laugh so easily. I was amazed that someone who knew so much pain in life could almost always find something to laugh about.) As a teacher, I would go in first. I would try to hold back the tears, but I know they would flow as I watched you proceed in with your classmates. What a miracle that would have been. I can't say I don't feel cheated to have seen you come so close, but not make it. I guess it will be in heaven before I understand why God did not let you graduate. I may not know why, but I do know that He does not make mistakes. The course that God had laid out for you to run was finished. You finished that course as you had faced life, with courage, grace and love.

Zach, I have gone over in my head hundreds of times what I would have said to you on your graduation day. To be honest, I would have written you a letter knowing that my emotions would never let me verbalize all that I feel. I am trusting God that somehow He will let you know what I am writing today.

I am so proud that you are my son! Before you were born, I dreamed of watching you play football and baseball. I dreamed of seeing you grow up playing all the sports I had loved. I dreamed of being able to coach you and see you excel as you grew up. God, in His wisdom, had different plans. I hope you know that you were never a disappointment to me. I could not be prouder of the man you grew up to be. I would not trade the man you became for all the athletic accomplishments and honors in the world. You left me, and so many others, a shining example of what is important in life: a love for God; a love for your family; a passion for the gift of life; a spirit that never gives up, no matter the struggles; a heart that never despairs, but always trusts and hopes. As God often does, He molded you, Zach, into someone far beyond what we had hoped our son would become. I say it again, I could not be prouder. I am honored to be your father.

Here are a few of the things I love about you Zach:

*Your courage. How does a teenager live for two years, knowing he may die any time, and not be totally consumed with bitterness and anger?

*Your passion. Everything you did, you gave it your all.

*Your love for your family! Your physical condition limited your peer relationships, but we benefited. Your best friends were your family!

*Your pride in your brothers. Because you could not play, you did so vicariously through Kemper and Cole. You were always there to cheer them on. Maybe they did not realize it, but everyone else knew how much you loved them and how proud you were that they were your brothers. We won't let them forget.

*Your sense of humor.

*Your love for people. You never met a stranger. You always had time to listen and talk to people, no matter who they were. You were a lot like Jesus in that way.

*Your love of God. I was privileged to be not only your dad, but also your youth minister and teacher. You had the kind of relationship with God that showed in how you faced life and how you treated people. I saw an intimacy between you and your Abba that few teens ever experience.

I could say more Zach, but we have eternity to talk. I'll wait until I see you face to face. For now, know that I love you! You were more than just my son. You were my teacher and my best friend. I miss you! The memories are sweet, but they will never replace the real thing. I can't wait until I see you. Let's play 18 together. Maybe somewhere like Pebble Beach. You always loved the ocean. I was going to say I'd let you drive the cart, but why don't we walk instead. It will be awesome!

I LOVE YOU!!!!!!
Dad

My prayer—Hebrews 4:16
"Let us then approach the throne of grace with confidence, so that we may receive mercy and find grace to help us in our time of need."

Thursday, May 27, 2004 6:35 AM CDT

We received Zach's diploma yesterday. It is an unreal thing to look at something that Zach should have been here to receive. These will be our last tangible things to treasure. I look at his senior pictures and I just cannot believe he is not here. The valedictorian spoke of Zach in his speech. He said that Zach, Z-man, loved everyone and didn't have any enemies. He said that Zach would always be the inspiration for the class of 2004. I hope & pray it is true. Carla

Sunday, May 30, 2004 3:52 PM CDT

I am glad that the last couple of weeks are behind us. Now, I sense the "flatness" from before. You go about life, but it is flat. You want to feel excited about something but it's not there. You want "this" to be gone. You want to feel normal (what ever that is). But, you don't. Everything in life seems tiresome. I function but sometimes by rote and nothing more. I am just tried. You know how when you're really tired everything seems to be overwhelming. That's how it is now. The tasks of life seem too large at some moments.

Hanging by a thread,
Carla

Permanent Sackcloth

It probably sounds like I am severely depressed, but really, when I think about life, I mostly think "Who cares?"
—Carla

Thursday, June 3, 2004 7:31 AM CDT
It seems like it will never be over. At moments I find that I smile or laugh at something and then there it is—the reality that Zach is gone. It seems that my mind cannot get a handle on that fact that Zach is gone from this life. I will think, "I can't believe it's over. I can't believe that Zach has lived his life and is gone. I can't believe this is the way it ended. I lived in fear of it for years but then it happened. Just when we thought we had hope, he was gone.

The other night Kemper said something and had an expression just like Zach. I thought my heart would break in my chest. I so wanted to reach out and it be Zach. I wanted to hug him. I can't seem to take in the whole thing.

I asked Johnny last night if I would ever feel passion about anything again. I loved to feel passion about what I do. Right now, I will think about something that I think I can be interested in or care about but then I say, "Who cares?" It is so strange. It is a strange way for me to live and feel. I just keep telling Jesus to carry me. I'm just going to sit in His lap until I feel better.

It has almost been 6 months and it still seems so unreal. At moments I think it's a bad nightmare. Surely this is not how it played out. I miss him so.

Hanging On, Carla

Saturday, June 5, 2004 5:40 PM CDT

It's been six months today. As I was out walking today I tried to just welcome all of the heaviness. I wanted to "feel" it. Cole said today, "Was Zach alive when we went to the beach last year?" It just hurt me. It's only been 6 months and Cole at age seven, can't really remember that last summer Zach was here.

I realize as we "go" on with life that our grief will become more internal. I was at work yesterday. Busy on the unit and there was a lot of activity & noise. All of a sudden in the background I heard the stereo playing, *I Can Only Imagine.* I was immediately at the memorial service for Zach. I was still in my seat at the desk, but really a million miles away. It was my private pain. I think that must be the way it is. It becomes more and more of an internal ache as life goes on.

I asked Johnny if he wanted to post and he said, "No, because I feel like I just keep saying the same thing. I just miss him so and it's so painful & lonely." I guess he is right. There are not many words just a lot of ache. I know there is no normal way to mourn, and there is no time frame that you can adhere to as time goes along.

Thanks for checking in on us.
Carla

Tuesday, June 8, 2004 11:18 PM CDT

I seem to deal with the same feelings day after day. During Zach's life, Carla and I both spent time imagining what it would be like if Zach died. We couldn't stay there long, for even in the contemplation the pain of losing Zach was incredible. In those first days after Zach died, the reality went beyond anything we imagined. Our previous contemplations of Zach's death actually helped us get through those first painful months. What we had never taken time to think through before though was how it would be six months after Zach died.

We are there now. The pain is not as intense as it once was, but it is still there. It is sort of like a tooth that's gone bad. You are aware of it as a dull sensation that is always present. Then, you drink something cold or hot and the pain

102

sends you through the roof. Everything else is dwarfed by the pain. You learn to be careful about doing certain things to keep away the intense pain. I try to protect myself from things that I know will trigger the intensely painful grieving. The grief is mostly like a wet blanket right now that covers everything else. My passion for anything is just not there. At best, the things that I used to enjoy are distractions from the pain.

There are some things that always trigger the grief. Cole has moved to Zach's room. I am glad because it gives Cole a connection with Zach. It's hard because as I put him into the bed each night, it is a stark reminder that Zach is not there. I still wear Zach's watch every day. I miss his phone calls. I can't fix a meal without being sad. Even though Cole has taken over Zach's seat, there is still a huge emptiness at the table. I see his picture and wonder "What if...?" These past six months seem like six long years.

Looking for the light, Johnny

Thursday, June 10, 2004 7:42 PM CDT
It seems that Johnny and I both have an unbelievable amount of heaviness. I feel like something is sitting on my chest. It is just so yucky to have this heaviness all of the time.

The First Presbyterian Day School Alumni booklet came today. The last page is dedicated to Zach. It is precious pictures of Zach. There is one of Johnny, Zach and me at the senior night football game this past fall. It was one of the last pictures we had made together. It was a beautiful tribute, but I just want to scream "Why?" Yet, I know that what we call "life" is actually a shadow of what is to come. It is a piece, but not the whole. It is easy to imagine Zach with Jesus, but it is not easy to imagine what the rest of my earthly life will be like without him.

At moments I feel like King Solomon when he said that everything is meaningless under the sun. That really is the way it is right now. Most things are meaningless. It probably sounds like I am severely depressed, but really, when I think about life, I mostly think "Who cares?" For those who are around me, you know that I can laugh and cut-up, but it is the deep questions of life and what it is about that nag me.

With a heavy heart, Carla

Sunday, June 13, 2004 11:31 AM CDT

I wish I could say things are better but they are not. I feel like I'm going backwards. I feel so frustrated, angry, heavy, unhappy, and empty. I just feel overwhelmed. I want to be beyond where I am. I want to be graceful about this but I am not. I really want to just get in a hole and stay there. I have this picture in my mind of what I look like. I am this tiny ant with my hands on my hips (if ants have hips) and I am telling God how it is. Even though I know how ludicrous it is, I am still doing it. I don't want to be here. I want to be where it says in Psalm 30:11-12 that God removes my sackcloth and clothes me in joy. I am not there. I am still wailing and sitting in the junk heap pile. God says He will turn it into joy. I am waiting. Carla

Thursday, June 17, 2004 5:24 PM CDT

Psalm 30:11-12 says, "You turned my wailing into dancing; you removed my sackcloth and clothed me with joy that my heart may sing to you & not be silent."

As I said the other day, I am waiting. I am not there yet. I feel like I may have permanent sackcloth in my closet. It seems it's the only thing I can wear. Even when I want to wear something not so heavy and ugly it jumps right on me. I would like to burn these clothes. It is the most exhausting, lonely, sad, miserable work I have ever done.

Today, for what ever reason, the grief has laid on me like a wet blanket. The emptiness and flatness is unbelievable. I feel like a walking zombie. I realized today I could not even laugh. It was too much effort. For some reason part of the process and healing must come as you wade through all of these heavy times. Maybe it will make the other side better. I don't know yet. I am not there.

Wishing for new clothes, Carla

Tuesday, June 22, 2004 1:02 AM CDT

Father's Day was about what I figured it would be...
HARD! I tried to focus on enjoying the time I had with
Kemper and Cole. The constant thought I had though was
that Zach wasn't there. These first time experiences without
Zach are so hard. The thought of his absence drowns every-
thing else out.

Two thoughts seem to always be with me. First is that I
miss him so terribly. Carla and I talked about the things we
missed most about him. Some were the same; others were
unique to one of us. As time passes, the magnitude of our
loss becomes more and more clear. The second thought is
struggling with the concept that I probably won't see him
again for a very long time. It always seems if I will be seeing
Zach soon, as if he just is not with us now. But then the
truth invades that fantasy and the reality is painful.

Only God can turn our mourning into dancing. He will
dry our tears. God brings the joy that follows the night of
weeping. Where we find ourselves is not because of something we have not done. It is the path of grief; the greater the
loss, the deeper and longer the grief. God is honored as we
continue to trust Him in spite of what our feelings tell us. It
is precisely that hope we have in God that distinguishes our
grief from that of a lost person's grief. We can embrace the
loss and pain knowing that one day God will lift us out of the
grief. One day, we will see our loved ones again. Without the
hope we have in Christ, I don't know how someone gets
through this. It is hard enough with Christ.

Johnny

Monday, June 28, 2004 7:02 AM CDT

This process continues to roll and pitch along. I am
always amazed by the phases of the grief. I realized that as I
make some progress (well I guess its progress) I will have
what I call some normal minutes. Then, all of a sudden a
"panic" type feeling hits that I am "losing" touch with my grief
and that some of it is sliding and slipping away. The grief is
the last tangible thing I have of Zach. It is strange how
"uncomfortable" the feeling is when you realize what is hap-

105

pening. As much as I want not to feel bad, I fear when the loss becomes a piece of the past.

I thought yesterday how much I want to be able to look in Zach's eyes and have him tell me that he is ok. I know that he is. But, my mother's heart wants to pull him over to the side and get the real story. Just like when you're in a group and you look at your child and know something is not right. You need to get them off to the side to get the real story. I want Zach to be able to tell me. I want to know if he is disappointed that he didn't get to go to Auburn. I know what the answer is but I still want to look in his eyes and see it. Missing Zach, Carla

Tuesday June 29th 2004 1000 AM CDT

One thought keeps coming to mind today. It is that "Life goes on." While Carla and I often want to just sit out for a couple of years, we are reminded that even as we are in our grief, God has left us here for a purpose. First, and foremost, we have two sons to continue to raise up. I pray that we do as well with them as we did with Zach. I also know that it is part of God's purpose that we continue to testify to His grace and sovereignty. We also share in the purpose of bringing glory to God. That is what God is all about. I hope and trust that God will continue to use us as His vessels of grace and mercy. Thank you again for being the hands, arms, and feet of Jesus as He continues to carry us through these days. We are blessed by you.

Looking unto Jesus, Johnny & Carla

Empty Beach & Empty Hearts

The work of grief and pain is hard enough without fighting the only One who can soothe my soul.
                                                                      —Carla

July 5, 2004 0:58 AM CDT

A year ago, Carla , the boys and I spent the 4th of July in Washington, D.C. Zach had spent the previous 2 weeks at a conference there. We had always talked about how cool it would be to spend the 4th in our nation's capitol. We had a great time as we sat beneath the Washington Monument and watched the fireworks display. I think none of us will ever forget it.

The thing that struck me was how quickly life can change. Last 4th of July, I never thought I would spend this year's 4th grieving my son's death. Week by week you hear of tragedies that befall people you know. It reminds me how precious each day is. How important it is to focus on the things that really matter. Jesus told us to live each day for that day. How many times do we find ourselves just trying to get through the day rather than seeing that day for the gift that it is? Even as I grieve, may God help me to see the love and the beauty that can be found in each new day.

Clinging to my Abba, Johnny

Wednesday, July 14, 2004 0:38 AM CDT

I can already tell that next week will be a hard one. As our family gets ready to go to the beach on our family vacation, Zach is always at the forefront of my mind. Our summer beach trip was one of Zach's favorite weeks of the year. He loved having all the family together in one house. Three years ago, we had to cancel our trip as we were in California with Zach in heart failure. As he recovered, rescheduling the beach trip was foremost in Zach's mind. We ended up missing a week of school for our beach trip. I can already feel the emptiness that will permeate the beach house with Zach not being there. I found myself crying each of the past two days as I was getting things together for the trip. I hear him and see him in my mind, but I can't hold or touch him. I would give anything if I could. This year will be hard.

I know the first time we go through special times without Zach will be the hardest. I also know that the summer beach trip will never again be quite the same. I love you Zach! I miss you so much!

Wishing for what cannot be, Johnny

Thursday, July 15, 2004 8:02 AM CDT

I wish the tears would flow. It seems like I cannot cry now. I have not cried in several weeks. I want to. It is a release when my tears flow. I feel backed up now. I do not know why I'm not crying. Even when you would think I might cry, I do not.

As Johnny mentioned the other day this next week on vacation will be interesting. It will be the first time we make family memories without Zach. A part of me wants to resist this. I don't want to move on. Another part of me knows that this is the way it is to be, but what about when we have more memories and events on the other side without Zach? What about when the memories with Zach fade. It is like you're torn between holding on and also wanting and glad to be at a place that is not so painful.

I think I have moved from my mind thinking (I cannot believe he died) to a subconscious sense that he is not here. Not a total reality but right below the surface. Maybe this is the progression the mind makes.

I was reminded this week that I am so grateful that I am at a place where I want and need Jesus to carry me. I am not fighting Him. I know that ultimately I have no hope of anything outside of Him. The work of grief and pain is hard enough without fighting the only One who can soothe my soul. Carla

Johnny & Carla-
I claim that I read the site to better pray for you, but I gen-
erally get so inspired by your words of faith and your incredi-
ble honesty. What a testimony you are. You're so open with
your feelings and struggles (and I truly can't even imagine
how painful & intense they must be) but you never fail to turn
to Jesus with these burdens. I think it would be so easy to just
give in to Satan's offer of pity & depression and just wallow in
the pain. But you two are digging deep and pleading with our
Lord to give you not only the strength to get through each day
(which has to be a major task) but you also have the foresight
to continue lifting your marriage and children/parenting up to
Him. I admire your hearts, which while they're breaking and
screaming at you to just quit; you keep offering them up for His
glory.

—Laura

Sunday, July 25, 2004 0:04 AM CDT

We are back from the beach. The week was everything I
thought it would be. It was great to be with family, but it was
one of the most painful and emotionally difficult weeks I have
had in awhile. I found myself going back to the days when
Zach's death was always at the front of my mind from when
I woke up to the moment I fell asleep. Thanks for the prayers
that I know were being lifted for us this past week.

Some of the most difficult times for me are when the family is together. Zach so loved our family get-togethers. When
we meet now, it magnifies Zach's absence to me. A whole
week of that was very difficult. I went for a walk the first day
we got to the beach. I spent an hour remembering past trips
and crying. I hate the reality that they will never be together
again this side of eternity. I want to scream!!! The long night
of grief continues on.

Hurting, but trusting, Johnny

Tuesday, July 27, 2004 7:12 AM CDT

From Johnny's posting it appears that the week was terrible. I think that he had the hardest time. It seemed like the week really threw him back into very intense grieving. I had a combination week. At times Zach's absence was so painfully real. I just could not believe he was not with us. I could just see him in my mind from last year. He so loved the week. I also had times that the tears flowed, which for me was good. I guess I better watch when I say the tears have stopped. They began to flow freely over the last week.

I did enjoy my time with my family. It was bittersweet. We would laugh and I would think about how hard Zach would have been laughing. One time King said, "The best thing about the beach is that you can find sand in your underwear a week later." Zach would have laughed until he could not catch his breath. He laughed at King (even if he was not funny). It was hard to really grasp that we will not ever have all of my family together again, on this side of heaven.

Kemper also had a couple of times where he talked about Zach and cried. I think he probably needed that also. It was a week of very mixed emotions and many firsts. The firsts are hard. Hanging On,

Carla

Thursday, July 29, 2004 7:21 AM CDT

I wanted to share a part of a beautiful tribute from a song that a friend wrote after Zach's death.

Fly Home (as we remember awesome Zach Morton)

We feel our painful limits - unable to see beyond this earthly horizon. But we know, even as he disappears, he is becoming greater as he flies toward those receiving him beyond the horizon... They are greeting him with a great celebration. "Well done my good and faithful one," the Creator says with tender power in His voice. "Welcome to the land of the living. Welcome to the home for which you were created."

I love the part about straining to see beyond the horizon. The pain we feel is because we cannot see beyond the horizon. We are limited. It is this pain that remains. I know where Zach is but I strain to get a glimpse beyond the horizon. Most moments I focus on where Zach is, but at unexpected times the staggering reality of his absence in "this field" is so intense it takes my breath away.

May God continue to "tend our field" here where we cannot see beyond the horizon but must believe.

Straining to See, Carla

Sunday, August 1, 2004 8:12 PM CDT

The school annuals arrived this week. The annual was wonderful but very bittersweet. The dedication page to Zach was great as were his senior pictures, senior ads and a final farewell. I found myself looking at the graduation pictures and scanning for Zach just a split second before I realized what I was doing. These are the last tangible reminders we have of Zach and his life here with us.

Hanging On, Carla

I've come to the conclusion that I cannot really convey in words what I feel when I think about Zach (which occurs daily, if not hourly). Today, reading your most recent journal postings and looking at the rendering of Zach's building, I found myself sitting in my office crying. Yes, literal rivers running down my face and dripping on my shirt. I think what moved me most was Zach's senior quote.

—Seth

Tuesday, August 3, 2004 11:55 PM CDT

As Carla mentioned, the FPD yearbooks came in last week. Looking through the annual was hard, but I was also very proud as I remembered what an awesome son we had in Zach. As someone once said, Zach represented everything that was good about the school.

It is hard thinking that if Zach had not died that he would be getting ready to go to Auburn. But then I am reminded that Zach graduated to something much better

111

than going to college. He had always dreamed of being an Auburn Tiger. He was so excited when he received his acceptance letter. As much as he dreamed of going there though, I know he would never give up the joy he is experiencing this moment. I was reading back over Zach's journal entries before I posted this. He mentioned that he got some pajamas for the hospital before the surgery. The shirt read "Wake me when it's over." I wonder if Zach ever dreamed about the glory he would awaken to.

The grieving continues. We miss Zach so much it hurts. But we have a hope in Christ that does not disappoint or fail. It is that hope that carries us through the night. Thank you God for the promise we have in Jesus! I can't wait until the hope and promise are fulfilled!

With Hope, Johnny

Friday, August 6, 2004 11:10 PM CDT
Yesterday marked 8 months since Zach died. These have been the longest 8 months of our lives. We know that in the light of eternity these past months are like a blink of the eye. Being here in this world, times of grief seem to slow everything down. I am still amazed at how quickly your life can be changed forever.

Resting with my Abba, Johnny

I heard a great message on Sunday that made me think of you all. It was a series on igniting your faith. The minister asked what our lives would look like if we really believed that God is who He said He is. How would we live if we really believed that God could be trusted? Your lives are examples of that! Your faith is so encouraging. In the midst of the pain, you have turned to Jesus instead of away.

—Mel

Memories of Zach

*Zach was an outstanding example of enthusiasm and
perseverance. Although he was often winded from activity,
he never took advantage of any special treatment offered.*
—Mrs. Caroline

Tuesday, August 10, 2004 11:43 AM CDT

I wanted to share another bittersweet honor we were
given last night. Covenant Academy, where Zach went to
school from Kindergarten through the 9th grade, dedicated
their 2004 annual to Zach. I wanted to share what was written as the dedication to Zach. It was written by Mrs.
Callahan who was Zach's first grade teacher at Covenant.
She also taught Kemper and had Cole in her first grade class
this year when Zach died. Mrs. Callahan read this tribute
about Zach at the dedication last night.

My Memories of Zach Morton
by Mrs. Caroline Callahan

*It was my joy to teach Zach in the first grade, my first year
at Covenant. I will remember his bright, broad smile and the
distinct brightness of his eyes! Zach was an outstanding
example of enthusiasm and perseverance. Although he was
often winded from activity, he never took advantage of any
special treatment offered. He was eager to do all he could do
and he certainly did. I remember how smart he was and how
strong he was in math.*

*Even at the tender age of six, Zach's trust in God was very
evident. He expressed real interest in and knowledge of the
Bible lessons. Probably the tenderest memory I will always
hold in my heart was on the last day of school when we had*

113

a special season of prayer for Zach. We knew he faced the possibility of surgery. He sat in my lap and all of his classmates gathered around us on the floor as we prayed and committed him to the Lord and His care and asking Him to make a way for Zach. How faithful He was to allow Zach twelve more years for us to observe his faith, growth, strength, and perseverance and God's faithful hand upon him.

This year Cole, Zach's youngest brother was in my first grade class. It has been special to get to know Cole as well. Zach would pick Cole up from school and this gave me the opportunity to get reacquainted a little. I was pleased to discover that Zach had grown into a dear, caring, and responsible young man. I am privileged to have known Zach and to see God's hand in his life. He will always hold a special place in my heart and my prayers of thanksgiving to God for allowing such a special person to cross my path.

Thursday, August 12, 2004 8:08 AM CDT

Yesterday I had to take Cole to Atlanta for his cardiac check-up. On the way up he said, "I don't want to go." I said, "I know but we need to." He said, "I don't even care about my heart. I don't care if I die." I told him that I understood but I wanted him to stay here awhile longer. It is obviously still on his mind about his heart problem and dying. Dr. Jones said that Cole is about the same. We are just holding steady at this point. Dr. Jones said that there will come a day that we have to do the surgery but not right now. I was grateful for that. I hope and pray that we can get a little time before we have to tackle that mountain.

I could tell that seeing us is hard for Dr. Jones. He said that he thinks about Zach a lot of the time. He said that he will never have another patient like Zach. Then he said, "But, you know I don't think I want to. I care about my patients but I don't know that I want to ever feel that way again." His eyes filled up when he talked about Zach.

It feels so strange, to go and not "feel" like I am loaded with questions, concerns, thoughts, suggestions. I always had a list of things to go over with Dr. Jones (since he saw both Zach & Cole). So much of my "job" is done. It seems like

I should be doing something more.

Grateful for the "reprieve," for the moment with Cole. Still struggling to find my "new" place in life. Carla

The fact that our children's lives make a difference and impact others for great good is what every parent hopes for. Zach's life made a difference. His friendship and acts of kindness enriched the lives of everyone who knew him; somehow just being with him made you feel better about yourself. May our Abba somehow use that knowledge in the process of bringing healing to your wounded hearts.

—Steve

Thursday, August 19, 2004 7:52 AM CDT

It seems at times I feel just numb again. Not exactly, the way it felt the first few months when it is shock & numbness, but a kind of flat evenness. It is like you can never really get back to where you were. I realize as days go by and life moves on that I still will never be the same. To many of those around me they might not notice, but I am not the same on the inside. It's not particularly good or bad it's just different. But, different feels strange. Like a part of me is forever gone or altered. What made me "tick" before seems gone. I seem to really be straining to fully remember & think about everything that Zach said to me at the very end. I guess it's a kind of holding on.

Hanging On,
Carla

Straining to See

Z-Man's Rules for Life

* God is your first priority.
*People are more important than winning. Relationships last.
* No whining. There is always someone worse off than you.
*Whatever you do, do it with passion.
*Never give up. There's always hope!

—*Zach*

Monday, August 23, 2004 11:21 AM CDT

I had the most bizarre dream this weekend. I dreamed that Zach had not died but that he had been on a wilderness trip. In my dream, it seemed so real, we could not believe that we had messed up and thought that he had died. We were so thrilled. I could see him so clearly. (My biggest concern in the dream was who we had buried) I woke up and for a moment had this excited anticipation that something good had happened. I guess I thought for a second that it was real and Zach was here. I guess that's about where I am now. That somehow it was all a very bad dream and a big mix up.

Life goes on but the inner ache remains. I am grateful that Zach is very much alive. Really more than ever before, but I strain and want to see him. I live in the moment & then relive it with "What if Zach was here?"

Straining to see, Carla

Thursday, August 26, 2004 11:57 AM CDT

It seems that so many things have happened that have me thinking "What if?" and when I do, the tears start flowing.

If Zach was alive, he would have started school at Auburn last week. From the time he was little he had dreamed of going to school there. If Zach were alive, we would be planning his birthday. He would have turned 19 on September

116

18th. We would have gone to the Auburn vs. LSU game that Saturday afternoon and then celebrated Zach's birthday and an Auburn victory. (I wouldn't bet on LSU that game. It being Zach's birthday and him with God's ear, I think Auburn will be tough to beat.) If Zach were alive, we would be talking all about the upcoming football season.

I miss Zach incredibly. It is an ache that won't go away. Memories are like someone holding a glass of water in front of someone dying of thirst and then pouring it out in front of them. Sometimes it as if I could reach out and touch Zach or hear his voice, but then he disappears. I so want to hear his laugh. I want to hold him. I want to be with him. This waiting to be reunited is the pits!

Looking for Jesus to come back! Johnny

Thursday, August 26, 2004 5:08 PM CDT

Cole is sleeping is Zach's room. We have left everything the same but he is sleeping in there. When I lay down with him at night, I look around the room and still cannot really grasp that Zach is never coming back here. I said something to Cole about shifting a desk over to have it closer to the bed. I realized when I said it, that I would have to do something with the stuff on the desk & floor. It hit me.........I had the split second thought that I would put Zach's stuff away. Then I realized what I had just thought. The reality that he does not and will not ever need it again hit me.

I thought about a statement I had heard before. It said "The soul of man will rest with nothing short of the Rock of Ages" That is so true. There is no rest for my soul outside of Jesus. Nothing else will satisfy. I now know that. All of life moves on as does the work of grief.

Finding Rest, Carla

Wednesday, September 1, 2004 8:40 AM CDT

I was lying in Zach's room last night (where Cole is sleeping) and I was thinking how it is so hard to put your finger on how you feel. On the one hand, I am very scared that it seems like Zach is slipping from me. I wonder if I feel that way now what about in 5 years. I want it to be fresh but at the same time I would like to feel "normal." I will have one moment where I feel that things are finding a new norm and then in the same split second I feel scared that I thought it. I realize that you could not function ever if you had to feel the way you do the first weeks and months. You can't live like that. But, I also want the sense of Zach's presence or I guess his absence to feel powerful. At first you are aware every second that Zach is gone. Then, it is like his very absence is so real it is almost tangible. Yet with time it begins to change. It is not as tangible that he is gone. There is a real struggle inside to "merge" the two desires & emotions. This may sound very confusing but I guess in a way that's because it is. Every day brings new changes & adjustments to the grief. It is still a very tiring work.

Hanging On, Carla

Friday, September 3, 2004 11:59 AM CDT
I did not anticipate how hard yesterday would be. Kemper had his first football game of the season. This time last year, at Kemper's first game I have one of the last pictures of myself with all of the boys. A friend had taken it after the game. I could never have imagined what the next year would bring. I did not realize how much I would ache for Zach yesterday. Cole asked this morning if Zach knew that Kemper ran track last year. I said yes at first and then realized that no, that happened in the spring after Zach had died in December. I ached when I realized that this will become the pattern. Much of life will have happened after Zach left us. We will soon have a year of events and memories without him. I hate that.

Weary today, Carla

Monday, September 13, 2004 7:57 AM CDT
As we start the week of Zach's birthday, I found myself this morning still thinking. I can't believe this is how it ended. I wonder how long I will do that. Johnny & I both feel that the grief is intense once again. Johnny says that he can not say Zach's name or talk about him without crying.

Zach is still an encouragement to me everyday and I want-ed to tell you about it. Zach never complained or felt sorry for himself and I am striving to be like that. And once again, thanks for raising such a wonderful son who, even almost a year after his death, is still touching my life in a huge way every single day.

—*Ellen*

Thursday, September 16, 2004 0:19 AM CDT

"It's so curious: one can resist tears and 'behave' very well in the hardest hours of grief. But then someone makes you a friendly sign behind a window, or one notices that a flower that was in bud only yesterday has suddenly blos-somed, or a letter slips from a drawer... and everything col-lapses."

—*Sidonic Gabriell Colette*

How true. I think back to those first days after Zach's death and I wonder how we survived it. God gave us a calm and strength that belied our broken hearts. Now, months after Zach's passing, we find ourselves back in the valley. It is a place where the smallest thing, a song on the radio, a glimpse of a car, passing by a restaurant where you once shared a meal, can move you instantly from not thinking about Zach to having to pull off the road because you can't see through the tears.

We find ourselves not only missing Zach's presence, but also grieving what might have been. His 19th birthday, phone calls from Auburn, cheering for Kemper at football, his laugh, his smile, his hugs and high fives; I still find myself thinking, "How can he be gone?"

As I was thinking about how hard Saturday might be, I reminded myself that God never promised us one year with Zach much less 18 years. Even though we can't celebrate Zach turning 19, (How old are you in heaven?) I pray that God will give us a good day remembering Zach's 18 years. We are so thankful to God for the years he gave us! God is good!

Resting on the Rock, Johnny

119

I thought of Zach last night as I heard this line, "The only thing better than being in the center of God's will is standing in His presence."

—Judy

Monday, September 20, 2004 8:09 AM CDT
I think the time leading up to Zach's birthday was harder than the actual day. It is a comfort and a gift to us when others remember and let us know they care. It was fun to watch Auburn have a big win. I am certain the team thinks they pulled it out, but I can't help thinking that they had some help. Zach would have totally enjoyed the win. But, whatever he is doing I know far surpasses the best we have to offer here. We know as we move through the rest of this year that it will be very difficult because we will relive everything that happened in Zach's last months here. Carla

Saturday, September 25, 2004 1:43 PM CDT
We continue to hear stories of how God is using Zach's life story and this website to minister to and encourage people who are facing struggles of their own. We are grateful to God and honored that he would use us and Zach as His vessels of grace and encouragement. Thank you to all who continue to share Zach's story and to those who lift us up in prayer. God is faithful to answer. Thanks so much!
It's all about Jesus! Johnny

Lost in the Memories

*Grief is grief but I cannot imagine trying to live without
the certainly in my heart of where Zach is & that he is fine.
It is an anchor that my soul clings to.*

—Carla

Wednesday, September 29, 2004 10:30 AM CDT

It's hard to describe how I feel at this point. We are
almost 10 months into this grief journey. At moments it
seems as surreal as it did when it happened. At moments it
seems like it's been so long since I have been able to touch
Zach.

It's so hard to think about how just this time last year,
Zach was here and we had hopes for his future. We are getting down to the last of everything. We only have a few more
events before we will have completed a year without Zach. I
feel torn, you want not to miss Zach so deeply but you also
do not want everyone to forget. Of course that is one of the
many choices in life that we do not have. Life moves on
whether we want it to or not.

Hanging On, Carla

Friday, October 1, 2004 10:26 AM CDT

Today is our anniversary. We have been married 21
years. I looked at him this morning and said, "It's been a
rough 21 years!" That's the TRUTH! I am grateful that we
could not see the future. Only by God's grace have we weath-
ered the storms together. It has been hard. Unfortunately,
grief is not something that is lighter when you share it. You
each have your own grief to carry.

I read something today that put into words my perspective on life. "I have come to the place where I believe a yearn-

121

ing for heaven is one of the purposes and one of the privileges of suffering and of losing someone you love. I never had that yearning before, but I do now. You see a piece of me is already there. I now see in a much fuller way that this life is just a shadow of our real life—of eternal life in the presence of God." (*Holding On to Hope* by Nancy Guthrie) This is very true.

Holding On, Carla

Wednesday, October 6, 2004 6:59 PM CDT
I have often said during this grieving process that you never know what may set you off into an emotional tailspin. I have missed Zach so much this fall. I miss our conversations and discussions that undoubtedly would have focused on football right now. I am feeling apprehensive about the next two months. November 23rd, Kemper's birthday, will mark the day that Zach and I left for California. I know that each day I will relive the day that Zach and I spent together as we move closer and closer to December 5th. I don't want to forget those days, but I am not looking forward to them. It's like seeing something ahead of you that you know is going to be difficult and painful. You'd like to avoid it, but you know you can't. As we have for the past 19 years we will trust our loving Abba to carry us through. We could not make it without Him.

Staying close to Jesus, Johnny

Monday, October 11, 2004 9:00 AM CDT
Oh, man what a couple of days. It seems like the grief is almost new again. I think maybe because, we are reliving Zach's last days with us this time last year. It's like my mind is beginning to replay scenes that happened during those last days. I can't shake the overwhelming sense of loss and missing Zach. It's like I keep thinking if only we could go back to this time last fall and somehow change things. The mind must need to work through this because the slightest thing brings a past-memory or scene to my mind. I was leaning down telling Cole something yesterday and all of a sudden I had this flash back to when I came home from

122

California. I had bent down and told him that Zach had gone to be with Jesus. The pain of that moment almost a year ago was so intense. I was so exhausted yesterday with crying and heaviness. I guess this is part of what must occur. In a way I don't want to not feel it because once we pass the year mark I am afraid that everything will fade. I don't want it to. Such mixed emotions. Wow........this is painful work.

Feeling wounded, Carla

I heard this and it reminded me of Zach and why he was so special and had such impact on all of our lives. "You can't control the length of your life, just the DEPTH." Somehow Zach was able to understand those simple truths, which elude most of us, and live them out. He genuinely made you feel that whatever time you spent with him was special and important to him. And the truth is that we were the lucky ones. We are the ones cherishing the moments spent with him.

—Steve

Monday, October 18, 2004 9:00 AM CDT

Yesterday was my birthday. Every event or special day is so hard. His absence is so tangible. I thought of him so often through out the day. Apparently, right before I woke up yesterday morning, I was dreaming and in the dream Zach was coming in the back door and at the same time the phone was ringing. His voice (it was so deep) was so clear as he hollered that "I will get the phone." It was so real. I so wish he had been coming home; although, he really is home. We're still the ones wandering around. We know these final weeks as we finish this first year without Zach, will be hard. We are grateful that so many are sharing this heartache with us.

Hanging On, Carla

Friday, October 22, 2004 10:46 AM CDT

It seems that the "flash backs" are increasing. I was thinking about something else this morning and all of a sudden it was a flash back to Dr. Hanley being called over the loud speaker to return to the unit when they were coding Zach. It's like post-traumatic stress syndrome, I guess, it just comes when you do not expect it. Then it is reliving what happened. It feels like a huge heavy blanket that has been thrown over me. I hate this feeling. It's like you need to fight it, but you're too overwhelmed to try. It's the fear of reliving the pain. You don't want to go there but your mind seems not to obey.

I suppose it's the time of year and leading up to the anniversary of leaving on the trip to California and ultimately to his death. At moments it seems as surreal as it did when it occurred. I know that the only way to survive is to run to Jesus and get in His arms and let Him carry me. But, the emotions are raw and still feel so painful.

Carla

Thursday, October 28, 2004 8:17 AM CDT

The other night I dreamed about the moments when we heard the call for the surgeon to return to the unit. This time in my dream, it wasn't Zach. When we got back into the unit, they told us Zach was okay, it was another patient. I awoke about that time. My mind & dreams seem to be reliving various parts of his last hospital experience but with a different ending. I find myself thinking, "But, what if he hadn't died? How would things be now? What would have happened in his life? What would our lives be like now?" I guess it's a part of the process. I have not done the "What if"s" before now. It seems if I control it during the day, that at night the unanswered questions fill my dreams.

Thanks for walking with us,
Carla

Tuesday, November 9, 2004 9:27 AM CST

I have hesitated to write because I think I will sound very schizophrenic. It is so hard to find words anymore to explain what I am feeling/thinking. I seem to be back to "numb". In some ways the whole thing seems surreal. Like I'm watching someone else do this and I am detached. I haven't been to the grave in probably 2 months. I just do not want to. Johnny is at a place where to talk or think about Zach makes him cry & hurt. He doesn't want to.

We are in the final days counting down the last times we had in this life with Zach. This time last year we were preparing to leave November 23rd. I honestly did not think he would die. I thought maybe they would say again that they could not do anything, but I really did not imagine him making it through what they called a very successful surgery and then dying. I get scared when I think maybe I haven't grieved yet, maybe I'm still in denial and I will have it all before me. (That is an overwhelming thought). Somehow I can still not get my mind and emotions around it. Maybe this is the heavy weariness of grief that you never "get it done." I love getting things done so something that can't be completed and checked off gets on my nerves.

I realize also that the holidays will be a "pain" for a long time. It's just that I don't want to do it. I don't "feel" like doing any of the things you do. I hate it that this time of year every year will be the time we lost Zach. I had always hoped and prayed that if we did lose Zach it would not be near Christmas. December 5th is pretty much smack in the middle of all of it.

Hanging on, but not really wanting to, Carla

Monday, November 15, 2004 8:18 AM CST
For those of you who know how Zach loved Auburn, Saturday was a Big day. The game had "Zach" written all over it. (Sorry Georgia fans). Johnny loves and is passionate about Georgia. He and Zach use to go at it all the time. Since Zach has died, Johnny has gotten an Auburn shirt and some orange clothes. He wore his Auburn shirt to watch the game. I thought maybe having been a Georgia fan for so long and now wearing Auburn colors and pulling for them might bring on some sort of breakdown.........

Johnny and Zach had talked last year about the Georgia, Auburn game this year. Zach wanted to meet and go together. (He had hoped and planned on being at Auburn) It is a painful, empty memory for Johnny.

As we finish these last days I am going to try & pull my thoughts together & share some of the things we have learned over this year.   Carla

Thursday, November 18, 2004 10:47 PM CST

I am afraid that the November 23rd will forever be tied to Zach's death in my mind. It is Kemper's birthday but also the day Zach and Johnny left last year. When we asked him what he wanted to do on his birthday he said "Nothing." I think he may remember that as the day Zach left home for good.

I ache to hear his voice. I want to hug him and hold him close just one more time. I want to pick up the phone and hear him say "What'cha doing?" I want to hear him laugh; to hear him call Cole "monkey." Just thinking about these things brings that ache that sticks in my throat and makes it hard to breathe or swallow. I want the day to come when I can think about my son without it hurting so much.

In all the pain I cling to the hope we have in Christ. I want to be mad at God, but I can't. I can't hold anger when I know His love. It is that love that keeps me going. I live day by day knowing that each one brings me one day closer to Him and Zach. I hope the days are not too many.

Clinging with hope, Carla

Monday, November 22, 2004 10:31 AM CST

I heard someone talk about how sometimes the way God will gain the most glory is not in the way we wanted the "miracle" to happen. I know that must be true with Zach. God could have certainly gained glory from a physical healing of Zach, which is what I wanted and hoped for but the greater glory must be occurring in taking Zach home. I wish it was different, but there is a peace and certainly in my soul about it.

Grief is grief but I cannot imagine trying to live without the certainly in my heart of where Zach is and that he is fine. It is an anchor that my soul clings to.

This day last year, Zach's class gave him a surprise "send off." He was so blown away. There was a big crowd and a cook out and a bon fire. It was great. The look on his face was priceless. Several people had gotten a video tape together with individuals, coaches, teachers etc. saying something to Zach about his up coming surgery. They had also arranged

126

for some of the Auburn football players to say something to Zach and wish him well. Even Auburn's coach was on the video. I thought Zach might just float out of the room when they showed him the video and those players came on and talked to him. It was absolutely priceless. He really did leave with a beautiful send off. I know he must have felt loved that night. I would not trade that memory & that night for anything. What a blessing it was for him and us. Zach kept saying "Now, don't let anything happen to this tape while I'm gone." It was like gold to him. I have not watched the tape since then. I don't know when I will be ready to hear all of the well wishes and the come back soons.

We left for the Atlanta train station last year on November 23rd. It was our last trip as a family. The boys and I said goodbye to Johnny and Zach as they started the trip to California. The memory is so vivid; Zach hugging Cole goodbye and sort of giving Kemper a sideways hug. I wish I could reach into that scene in my mind & bear hug Zach again.

Thanks for sharing these lasts days of this first year journey with us.

Carla

Freedom

I walked in on Carla and Zach as she was just holding him. The image reminded me of "The Pieta," the sculpture and painting of Mary holding Jesus after his death. It was such a picture of loving tenderness, almost a holy moment. Zach had a spirit that could not be contained by that frail body. In an act of love God set him free.

—Johnny

Wednesday, November 24, 2004 8:14 PM CST

I find myself crying frequently as I remember the last days I spent with Zach. The remembering is both sweet and painful. I don't want to miss any of it. I almost feel cheated because Thanksgiving comes two days earlier calendar wise. I want to remember everyday we spent together.

At a conference last weekend, one of the speakers talked about how we need to embrace the "desert" experiences God brings us to. It is in the desert that God makes us thirsty for Him. It is in the desert that we learn to depend on God. It is in the desert that we learn that life is all about God, not about us. Moses spent 40 years in the desert to prepare him for another 40 years in the desert. I hope I don't stay here that long.

Thanks to all of you who have stayed with us this last year. I don't know that we would have made it without your prayers.

Smiling and weeping, Johnny

Saturday, November 27, 2004 1:40 PM CST

As much as we miss Zach, from time to time we are grateful that he is not here. Last night, FPD lost in the state championship football game by one point in overtime. If Zach were here, he would have been so bummed out. Zach's death also continues to put life in perspective. Losing a football game is hard, but there are tougher things in life we will face. That perspective is one of the great truths God has taught us in all of this.

These past days since Kemper's birthday have been hardest on me. Those were days that only Zach and I had together. Tomorrow will mark the day that Carla came and joined us. I am sure that she will begin to relive those last days with Zach as I have been doing. We cherish the memories, but reliving them this first year is so hard!

Lost in the memories, Johnny

Zach was born with such a unique heart—not only in the way we immediately think of— but in "matters of the heart." It's as if God compensated for Zach's heart "problems" by giving him an ABUNDANT measure of being able to give and receive love so openly and unconditionally.

I know that you miss him more than words could ever express. Thank you for sharing your "hearts" so openly with so many people. God has used you to minister to others by sharing your grief. I know that would never be something that any of us would choose, but your deep love for Zach is so evident, I know he would be proud of both of you for sharing that.
—Betsy

Monday, November 29, 2004 5:12 PM CST

I find myself being so irritated. I want everyone feeling what we are feeling. But, the reality is that some people I pass everyday will not even know that this is the week Zach died. It's the holidays & everyone is busy. I know in my heart that those who really matter the most to us know and care but somehow the whole world should be able to "sense" this. Today, someone said in passing that their child would be 20 years old tomorrow. Man was that painful. I will never know Zach as a 20 year old. I don't want people to tip toe around me, but sometime I want to scream.

I am in this place and time physically but emotionally I

am miles away re-living my own private pain. I guess I think it should be clearer at times what is happening on the inside but I guess its best that way. I've realized over this last year how personal pain is. There truly is a great chasm between the sufferer and others. Carla

Johnny & Carla,
Zach's life and the lessons he taught us continue to have lasting effects on so many lives. My class is studying God's sovereignty and living like Job did. Walking through this past year with you has colored my perspective on life here vs. our real home in heaven..
—Judy

Tuesday, November 30, 2004 11:37 PM CST

I am so heavy these days as I relive those last precious days we had with Zach. The emotion is so deep. Each day seems to bring the memory of the last time we did certain things with Zach. So much of our lives together were built around sports and that was the last event we ever shared together. How I miss those times!

Tomorrow, December 1st, was probably the hardest day we ever had with Zach, other than the day he died. It was on December 1st that Zach had the heart cath. It was that day that they told him of all the possible complications. It was on that day that we found out Zach had known he might die for the two previous years. If I close my eyes, I can still hear him crying in pain and anguish. We felt so helpless to ease his suffering. As I think about that day, I am filled with joy that Zach will never feel pain or fear again. We still hurt, but Zach never will again. Thank you God!!!!

I don't know what these next days will bring. I expect them to be hard. But I also know that God will be holding us every step of the way. He is faithful!

Trusting He's there when I can't feel Him,
Johnny

Wednesday, December 1, 2004 4:27 PM CST

I wanted to add my p.s. to Johnny's thoughts from last

night. As I went by the grave today, I was thankful that Zach was not where he was this time last year.

My heart aches when I remember the look on his face, when he told us he had known that he might die. In a way it seems crazy that we did not know, but Zach never, ever let on. He never talked about dying. He was just always about living. But, really when I think about it what is there to say about dying? I guess it is the fear of the unknown or what it will be like or what it will feel like. Apparently, Zach, for whatever reason, did not spend anytime dwelling on that.

One very tender, precious thing that happened that night is when we returned to the hotel late. We of course were totally spent. Zach was not to stand up long or to shower. He really wanted his hair washed though. So, I fixed it so he could just lean back on the tub while sitting on the floor & I could wash & rinse his hair without anything else getting wet. As, I was washing his hair he looked so tired, so thin, so blue (his actual color) and he was breathing so hard as he leaned back for me to wash his hair. I remember praying and thinking, *God I can't do this.* I hate to see him suffer. At that point the surgery seemed so horrible that no one in their right mind would agree to go through with it. (Based on what we had been told that evening.) Of course if he did not then he would continue to get worse and then die. I was so torn. I was glad though that I could "take care" of him. Do something for him. Take care of his physical needs that night. It's like God let me have one last time to "care" for him.

Forever that "bath" will be precious to me. I wish I could rub his short fuzzy hair right now. I do not wish him back in that body of his but I would love to just give it one Big Bear Hug. My tears are blocking my view so I will go. Please know that I am so very honored that so many pray & care. We are blessed to have encouragers along this road.

Weeping but knowing Zach is safe at last.
Carla

I'll add my P.S. now. I walked in on Carla and Zach as she was just holding him. The image reminded me of "The Pieta," the sculptures and painting of Mary holding Jesus after his death. It was such a picture of loving tenderness, almost a holy moment. Zach had a spirit that could not be contained by that frail body. In an act of love God set him free.

Johnny

I have read every entry you have made in the journal. I have been touched and God has used so much of what you have said to encourage me. Today, I wept...more that usual. What a tender picture. What a testimony. Zach is home now. He is safe. He is not bound by his earthly body. What a picture of God's love for us.

—Melanie

Jesus, the Anchor of Our Souls

How amazing it must be to know what we all wonder? Is it possible to describe or are there no words to do it justice? What does He look like? I know you can run now without getting tired...but can you fly, too? One day we will know just like you do now, but until then, tell everyone we said hello and we can't wait to see them...especially you, Zach. I miss you so much.

—Maggie

Friday, December 3, 2004 7:45 AM CST

I did not think this time last year that we would walk through the very heart of grief this year. I am only grateful that you all have chosen to walk with us and encourage us every step of the way. Thank you for allowing us to share our walk with you. We know that we have many, many more difficult painful days ahead as we walk in this life without our precious Zach. We are grateful though that you chose to share this first year with us. I do hope you will never forget Zach. I know he would be thrilled to know that you cared, missed him and were touched by his brief but very amazing life.

One night prior to going to California last year, I told Zach that it was like walking through a dark tunnel (where we were right then) we did not know what was in the tunnel but we knew what the light was at the end of the tunnel. Little did I know that the Light would call Zach home so quickly. Zach did run the race and finish with a "Well Done!" We are forever grateful for you walking through the tunnel with us. May God richly bless you.

Knowing we will be held,

Johnny & Carla, Kemper & Cole...& all of our wonderful family.

I have continued to be overwhelmed by your unswerving faith and testimony to the goodness and faithfulness of God, even in the midst of the most intense and devastating pain. I am stuck by your continued desire for what's best for Zach and rejoicing in his freedom from pain, even though it's brought intense pain to the two of you. And it occurs to me that the character traits that so amaze us about Zach are what we have observed in you this past year. And I see in all of this the living out of the truths found in Psalm 145:

"Great is the LORD and most worthy of praise; his greatness no one can fathom. One generation will commend your works to another, they will tell of your mighty acts. They will speak of the glorious splendor of your majesty, and I will meditate on your wonderful works. They will tell of the power of your awesome works, and I will proclaim your great deeds. They will celebrate your abundant goodness and joyfully sing of your righteousness....They will speak of the glory of your kingdom and speak of your might, SO THAT all men may know of your mighty acts and the glorious splendor of your kingdom. Your kingdom is an everlasting kingdom, and your dominion endures through all generations. The Lord is faithful to all His promises and loving toward all he has made."

This time a year ago Jesus fulfilled that promise for Zach, "I will...take you to be with me that you also may be where I am." (John 14:3) He took Zach to his eternal home. And with that act, He caused you and so many to become instantly "homesick". Although painful, that is not a bad thing.

Thank you for allowing us to tag along on this journey. Your ministry has been significant and impacted so many who you will never know this side of eternity.

You will continue to be in my thoughts and prayers. And along with you I will look forward to that day when December 5 will not be a day of intense pain and longing, but a day of celebrating alongside Zach, his birthday from the Shadowlands to the Light.

Much love,

—Steve

Sunday, December 5, 2004 9:47 PM CST

It is hard to believe a year has passed. Sometimes it feels like 10 years since I last saw Zach, but then, when you are hurting, it seems like they just told you he was gone. I think that strange juxtaposition will always be a part of our lives.

I know that many have been lifting us up these past days. Your prayers have been felt. The heaviness has been there all week, but not the intense pain I feared. My sister gave me a book about heaven by Randy Alcorn and I think that helped. I focused on the future I have with Zach in heaven, rather than the days in this time without him. It is that future promise that adds hope to our grief. Hurting, but hopeful, Johnny

You've shown us biblical grief, in honest and un-sugar-coated reality, but not without hope. And with that hope you've expressed the real gospel of our Lord Jesus Christ. That life on earth is not always fair, is not without hardship pain and suffering, and is not about health and wealth and prosperity. But, it's about loving and being loved, finding and being found, and ultimately about trusting the One who made us for Himself, fearfully and wonderfully, and has made a way and a promise to bring us Home.

—Steve

Tuesday, December 7, 2004 11:26 PM CST

In the days after Zach's death, Carla and I wondered if Zach knew he was going home to heaven. Were his last messages of love, sign language to Carla and me and the note to his brothers, Zach's way of saying goodbye? We won't know until we see him in heaven, but it made us think. Was he scared? Did he know that God would take him home that night? Our fear was that Zach would be upset after the surgery. We were so relieved when that proved to be untrue. He wasn't agitated or scared or even hurting. His only frustration seemed to be when he wanted to tell us something. We were so grateful that God gave Zach peace for the moment. As we look back we ask, "Was that dying grace?"

In the days and weeks ahead, we continued to wonder

about Zach's last hours. We wanted to know that he was OK now. I asked God to give me a dream that Zach was happy in heaven. Instead, God gave Larry, Carla's father, a dream about Zach. To be honest, I was ticked off at God. Why Larry and not me? I was Zach's dad! I had prayed for such a dream!

One afternoon, as I was reading Joni Erickson Tada's book on heaven, I came to a chapter on angels. As I read the chapter, I thought about Zach's death and again wondered if Zach was scared or surprised. I had my eyes closed, asking God if angels were with Zach when he died when God gave me an incredible vision. I was in Zach's room in ICU at the hospital. There were no doctors in the room, just Zach. He was lying on the bed, but he was not hooked up to anything. He was wearing blue jeans and his FPD letter jacket. He seemed to be sleeping. I saw another figure and heard him say, "Zach, it's time to go. I'm going to take you home." Zach immediately got up and smiled that big Zach grin. He seemed to know that "home" wasn't Macon, but his true home in heaven. He looked tan and healthy without a trace of blueness. He said one word in response, "Awesome!" Zach had the same look on his face that he did the first time he walked into Yankee Stadium or Wrigley Field. It was an expression of absolute rapture and pure joy! The other person took Zach by the hand and said, "I'm your guardian angel. I have been with you since the day you were born."

My next view of Zach and his angel was the two of them walking together. I saw someone approaching them and realized it was my dad. They both ran and hugged each other. I suddenly realized that my dad looked like he did when he was in his twenties and married my mother. After they embraced, my dad said to Zach, "I want you to meet someone. This is Jesus." I saw Jesus wrap up Zach in a bear hug and heard him say, "Welcome home little brother. Well done!"

The vision stopped. Tears ran down my cheeks as I thanked God for the gift He had given me. I don't know if Zach knew he was going to die, but I know he wasn't scared. I can still see Zach in his FPD jacket with that radiant smile and hear that familiar expression, "Awesome!" Yes it is!

Awaiting the upward call, Johnny

Friday, December 10, 2004 1:13 am est

A year ago today we buried Zach. The past year has definitely been the most difficult of our lives. As I reflect back, I still believe the things I said at Zach's memorial service. I thought it appropriate that I post what I had written for the service. I will post one last time later tonight. Thanks for sticking with us. Johnny

Zachary King Morton's Memorial Service
December 10, 2003
Ephesians 3:20

Now to Him Who, by the [action of His] power that is at work within us, is able to [carry out His purpose and] do superabundantly, far over and above all that we [dare] ask or think [infinitely beyond our highest prayers, desires, thoughts, hopes, or dreams]—

As Carla and I sat in the ICU, early last Friday morning, knowing that Zach was probably being taken home, Carla asked me: "What about all those people who have prayed for Zach? What will happen to their faith?" I want to assure you that God answered your prayers and even more. From the time Zach was a baby, thousands of people have been praying for his healing. We wanted Zach healed, to have a healthy heart and the ability to do the things that most of us take for granted. God had other ideas. God created Zach exactly the way he wanted him to be. It wasn't in spite of his defect that Zach grew into the special young man he was, it was because of the problems he had. It was his heart problem that opened the doors for Zach to live more in 18 years than most people do in 80.

There are other things I could share, but just know this: God answered ours and your prayers "superabundantly, far over and above all that we [dare] ask or think [infinitely beyond our highest prayers, desires, thoughts, hopes, or dreams]—" One last thing. Let me read this from a devotional by Steve McVey, President of Grace Walk Ministries. "Physical death is really just a gateway. In a sense we don't

137

really die. We just move from one location to another. Christians possess the life of Jesus Christ and His life is eternal. We simply one day leave what C.S. Lewis called "The Shadow-Lands" and move into the direct light of his glory. ...let's remember this fact—Christians don't die. We just go home and start the next chapter of the Divine Love Story which will never end. Earth introduces the characters. Heaven is the heart of the story."

Where We Are Today

Without Christ, I could not bear this life or especially Zach's death. As I grieve and live I do so with hope. I hurt for those people who do not have the hope that we have in Christ Jesus.

—*Johnny*

Summer, 2006

The bad news is that my grief is still alive and well. The good news is that my pain is less severe. I still have the "reality" hit me every morning as I plod to the kitchen to get my coffee. My mind is not still in shock, but it is a sobering reckoning each day that Zach is no longer here. Some days it seems like a distant painful event of the past, yet missing him is still fresh and ever present. Other days the pain is as intense as it ever was. I ache to be able to touch him and talk with him. Even when I have a moment of joy or pleasure, it is tempered by the keen sense of Zach's absence. I realize now that you can never go back. You can never reclaim what you have lost. You make a new reality to live with day by day. I was walking on the beach a few weeks ago. The fog had settled in and I could only see a few feet in front of me. I could hear the ocean; I knew it was there but I could not see it. As I listened to the sounds of the ocean, God spoke to my heart.

"This is where you are right now. You can only see a few feet in front of you and you can't see me at all. Trust me that I am here. Know that I am here. When you can't see a thing, keep walking!   Keep trusting!"

Still walking, still trusting,
Carla

To my firstborn,

Zach, it's been two and a half years since you left us. In a few months we'll celebrate your 21st birthday. Everyday Mom and I have to face the reality of life without you. Some days are harder than others, but we go on one day at a time. We learned that from you; take life one day at a time. Don't waste a moment.

The passing of time has lessened the pain. There are still those moments when it hurts so much I can't even breathe. Thankfully they are fewer of those moments. The thing that hasn't changed is the emptiness. The good times we have, family gatherings, Kemper's games and races, vacation, Cole's games, are wonderful, but your absence overshadows all of them. We don't always talk about it, but I know every-one feels it.

I think Cole has struggled as much as any of us Zach. You were such a huge part of his life. I know a day doesn't go by that Cole does not think about you. Thanks for being such an awesome big brother!

Kemper grieves as well, but I think in a different way than Cole. While Cole misses his protector, I think Kemper miss-es the friendship you all would have had. He misses a big brother to talk to as he goes through his teen years. He is an awesome athlete, tough as nails. How could he not be seeing how you lived life and faced death? A great part of his drive to succeed is that you could not play the sports you loved so much. When he plays or runs, he is doing it for both of you. Whatever he is doing you are there with him Zach.

I miss you Zach! I am so honored that I was chosen to be your dad. I trust that in God's grace, we will get a chance to make up in eternity what we lost here in this life. It is that hope that keeps me going. Until then, know that I love you. War Eagle!

Dad

Fathers Day – 2007

Today is Fathers Day. The pain is still with me. This day is always hard. I almost feel guilty about being sad and down. I am blessed with two wonderful other sons, but that joy is overshadowed by the pain of my firstborn not being here. That huge hole in my heart remains.

As I sat by Zach's grave today, I thought about some questions someone asked me not long ago. "What have you learned from these past years since you lost Zach? How have you changed?" I'll answer the second question first.

I have changed since Zach died. Carla tells me I don't laugh as much or as easily. That is probably true. As I have said before, even the most joyous of times are tempered by Zach's absence. She also complains that my gift giving skills have gone down the drain. A part of me died when Zach died. I realize that it was that softer part of myself and it bothers me because I know it affects those I love the most. Maybe it will return in time. I hope so.

What I've learned since Zach's death can be summed up in three points"

* All of life is about God and His glory. It is not about my happiness. I know that I will be most satisfied when God is most glorified in my life.

* We are created to spend eternity with God. This life I am living on earth is but a temporary existence that God will use to prepare me for eternity with Him. Zach's death has increased my desire to be with God. As Paul said, "To live is Christ, but dying is better still."

* Without Christ, I could not bear this life or especially Zach's death. As I grieve and live I do so with hope. I hurt for those people who do not have the hope that we have in Christ Jesus. It is best summed up in the words of Edward Mote:

My Hope Is Built on Nothing Less
by Edward Mote

My hope is built on nothing less
Than Jesus' blood and righteousness.
I dare not trust the sweetest frame,
But wholly trust in Jesus' Name.

When darkness seems to hide His face,
I rest on His unchanging grace.
In every high and stormy gale,
My anchor holds within the veil.

His oath, His covenant, His blood,
Support me in the whelming flood.
When all around my soul gives way,
He then is all my Hope and Stay.

When He shall come with trumpet sound,
Oh may I then in Him be found.
Dressed in His righteousness alone,
Faultless to stand before the throne.

On Christ the solid Rock I stand,
All other ground is sinking sand;
All other ground is sinking sand.

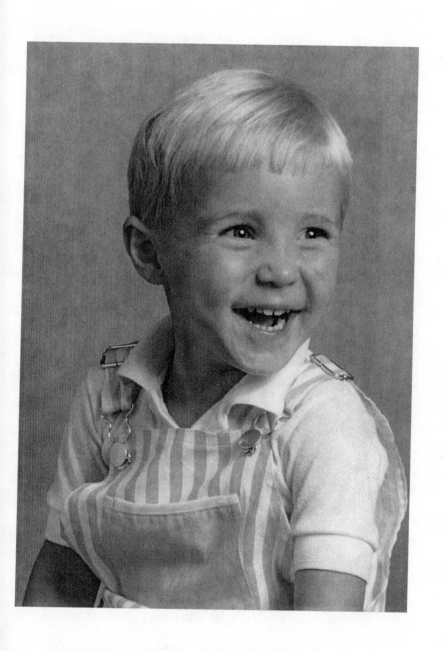

**As a two-year old,
Zach could light up the room with his smile.**

As much as Zach loved sports, his heart only allowed him
to play sports one year. Here he is playing T-ball at age
five. Because of the difficulty in breathing while playing,
Zach never played another sport.

Zach at age six—the ultimate Auburn fan.
Zach was set to attend Auburn in the fall of 2004.

Zach's favorite holiday was Christmas. He loved it
because we were together so much as a family.

**Zach, Carla, Kemper, and baby Cole
on our summer beach trip.**

Zach, 15 years old, with Dan Reeves,
head coach of the Atlanta Falcons at the time.

**Yankee Stadium welcome for Zach
on his 2001 Wish Trip.**

As we drove home from California in 2001,
Zach served as a ball boy for the L. A. Dodgers.

Zach and Johnny in the Dodger's locker room with starting pitcher, Kevin Brown.

Zach and one of his classmates, Ashley Griffin, at a going away party the night before we left for Zach's surgery.

Senior night for the FPD football team in 2003, our last photo taken with Zach. Zach kept stats for the team.

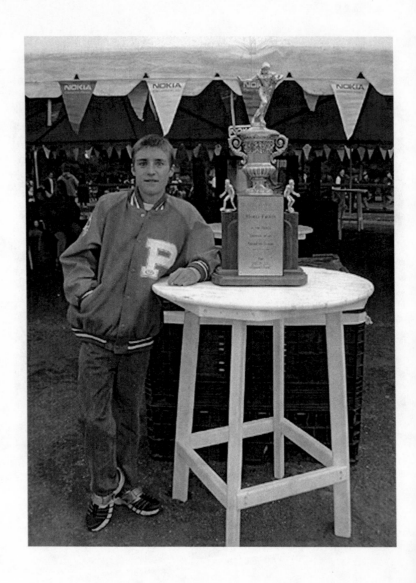

Zach, in his FPD letter jacket, before the Stanford-Notre Dame football game. It's the last picture we took of him.

Where We Are Today—Christmas, 2008

It's been five years since Zach stepped into eternity and we started this grief journey. Some days I still can't believe it really happened. Other days it seems so long ago. The intense pain is gone for the most part. In its place is a dull ache of missing Zach. Sometimes a season or event will trigger the sharp pain of missing him. It is Christmas time and it is hard. I wish he was here. I think about other families looking forward to their children coming home and it hurts. I try to imagine what he is doing and wonder if Zach thinks he has been gone from us a long time. I know that I will not know until l I get there.

What I do know is that this journey is about learning to walk by faith, not by sight. I know that God has anchored my soul in Him. It is not my faith that is the issue but the object of my faith. This journey has taught me how sufficient my God is. God can not be anything but faithful to His own. There are days I do not feel this, but I am choosing to believe it. I know that we would not have survived this journey without His grace and mercy every moment of every day.

My desire and prayer is that in sharing our grief journey, we have given you hope by pointing you to the One that will carry and comfort you in your grief. May we all be given the grace to walk by faith until that faith becomes sight.

We would love to hear from you and know if our journey has encouraged or helped you. Please feel free to visit us at our web site: www.noregretz.org

Still Believing,
Carla Morton

About the Authors

Carla and Johnny Morton have been married for over 25 years. Johnny is chairman of the Bible department at First Presbyterian Day School in Macon, Georgia where he has taught high school students for the past eight years. He has spoken at numerous retreats, seminars and conferences across the country. Carla has been a Registered Nurse for the past 25 years. She says that much of what she learned about compassion and caring in her profession came from being on the other side of the bed as a parent with Zach. She is currently completing her masters as a Clinical Nurse Specialist in adult health with a post-masters certificate in Nursing Education. Carla and Johnny have two other children, Kemper, age 18, and Cole, age 12.

Photograph courtesy of Larry Falls

The Mortons
Kemper, Carla, Cole, & Johnny

LaVergne, TN USA
15 June 2010
186201LV00001B/95/P